Buying and Managing Residential Real Estate

Second Edition

ANDREW J. McLEAN

McGraw-Hill

New York Chicago San Francisco Lisbon London
Madrid Mexico City Milan New Delhi San Juan
Seoul Singapore Sydney Toronto

The McGraw-Hill Companies

1 2 3 4 5 6 7 8 9 0 AGM/AGM 0 9 8 7 6 5

ISBN 0-07-146219-8

McGraw-Hill books are available at special quantity discounts to use as premiums and sales promotions, or for use in corporate training programs. For more information, please write to the Director of Special Sales, Professional Publishing, McGraw-Hill, Two Penn Plaza, New York, NY 10121-2298. Or contact your local bookstore.

This book is printed on recycled, acid-free paper containing a minimum of 50% recycled, de-inked fiber.

Contents

Preface

Welcome to the second edition of *Buying and Managing Residential Real Estate.* It's all about how to invest in single-family homes and small multiunit buildings and how to do it in your spare time, and without quitting your job. From making the first acquisition and showing and renting units, to pyramiding your investments, and retiring on your real estate holdings, this book is a complete and easy-to-read guide to smart, carefree investing.

I like to call real estate investing a "plant a seed and watch it grow investment plan" because you first acquire one property—the seed that will be the root of your future wealth—and increase its value, while at the same time sheltering wage income, thus allowing you more surplus money to invest in additional properties. Then you use income and appreciation generated from the "seed" property to acquire more realty investments. If you properly utilized the success-proven guidelines outlined in this book, you could, realistically, retire comfortably on your income-producing realty holdings alone.

It is *not* a get-rich-quick scheme or an impractical no-money-down scheme that you might see on late-night television for earning mythical millions overnight. Although I have included several proven no-money-down strategies for your consideration (see Chapter 4). It is, however, an easy to follow, methodical way of first acquiring one property, then fixing it up, and renting it (perhaps with an option for the tenants to buy) in contemplation of acquiring additional properties. And it features how to manage them efficiently without some of the hassles unskilled or new landlords can experience.

My Experience Is Yours for the Taking

Written in conversational style, the book couples my personal expertise in investing with a broad working experience in real estate. Over a span of 32 years, I have had the opportunities to not only do a lot of personal investing but also to work in a wide range of real estate–oriented professions. These have included working as a real estate appraiser, a property manager for a major developer, a loan officer, a foreclosure specialist for a 39-branch savings and loan, and a resident manager of a luxury 363-unit apartment complex.

But the book is more than just reminiscing about my varied experiences. It also blends my core principles with proven expertise to provide lessons for beginners or midlevel investors that they might not otherwise have. So, for instance, when you're buying a piece of property, this book answers the pertinent questions: How and where do I get a mortgage? How do I find good-paying, long-term tenants? How do I know if the real estate I'm looking at is a good deal?

This book answers many other questions too:

- What are the key guidelines to making a superior real estate investment?
- How do I negotiate profitably in real estate?
- What improvements should I make, and which ones should I avoid?
- What type of financing should I get—a fixed- or an adjustable-rate mortgage?
- What types of properties make the most profitable investments?
- How do I avoid deadbeats and find good-paying tenants who will care for my property?
- What are the best and most efficient methods for collecting rent?

How do I write an advertisement that will attract conscientious tenants? In addition, this book offers sound advice on

- Evaluating specific properties
- Shopping for the best mortgage loan to suit your particular needs
- Negotiating successfully and using high-powered negotiation tactics
- Earning great returns on a modest investment

This book doesn't tell you to just make sure you have enough money so that you're not underfinanced. It's easy to say: Don't be underfinanced. But what does the student or reader really get out of that? Not much. Instead, what the potential investor really needs to know is *where* do I get the money and *how much* do I need. How do I arrive at a business plan? What do I write? How do I make the business plan salable to my investors or to potential lenders? This book addresses those questions and many more.

The featured section of the book—guidelines to making a superior realty investment and hassle-free techniques to efficient property management—is styled from the Investing in Real Estate course I teach at the Jefferson Davis campus of the Mississippi Gulf Coast Community College. This is the true nuts-and-bolts section of the book, which the reader should find invaluable in any realty investment situation.

In the section on property management, you'll learn

- How to find quality tenants that pay on time and will care for your property
- How to take the hassle out of being a landlord
- How to maintain harmony by profiling your tenants
- How to overcome inflation and taxes
- How to use success-proven strategies to optimize income

You'll also discover in this book how to

- Find the best low-cost financing
- Avoid adjustable-rate mortgages and prepayment penalties
- Apply the two-points rule of thumb to know when to refinance your mortgage
- Negotiate a winning deal with high-powered tactics
- Utilize three key principles to maximize your investment
- Make improvements that pay, and avoid ones that don't
- Spot a real estate lemon
- Make profitable realty investments using the 11 key guidelines to making a superior investment

Other topics include critical dos and don'ts in evaluating a location to invest in. Among them are

- Be sure you have sufficient land for future expansion
- Always consider the logistics—location to and from work and shopping

The book also features worthwhile tips and highlighted "Landlord Tales," which are heartfelt stories and anecdotes from my personal experiences in real estate.

While the book is aimed primarily at beginning and midlevel real estate investors—owners of one or two rental properties—it will also be of interest to

- Anyone who is interested in owning his or her own home or investment real estate
- Anyone unsure of how to negotiate a real estate transaction
- Anyone who is interested in learning high-powered negotiation techniques
- Anyone who wants to learn how to appraise real estate
- Anyone who wants to learn hassle-free methods for attracting good tenants and optimizing profits
- Anyone who is unsure about what type of financing to choose
- Anyone interested in learning how retire on his or her realty investments

Do you like the concept of owning your own home and earning tax-free income and appreciation on your realty holdings as a successful landlord, without all the usual hassles other novice property owners experience? If you answered yes, then this book was designed for you. This is your spare-time guide to profitable realty investing and hassle-free property management.

With basic nuts-and-bolts guidance throughout, this book will serve as an excellent guide for both layperson and professional. Whether you're just getting started at investing or you are already a multiproperty landlord, you'll find a wide range of topics advising you on profitable investment opportunities. In creating this book, I have tried to cover all the angles and make it the all-in-one guide that covers everything you need to know to elude uncertainty and invest in today's real estate market—safely, confidently, and profitably.

Good luck with your realty investments.

Sincerely,

A. J. McLean

Introduction

Congratulations for taking the time and effort to discover the second edition of *Buying and Managing Residential Real Estate.* Since the first edition was published in 1988, communism collapsed in the USSR in 1991; the United States was attacked by terrorists on September 11, 2001; and mainland China, recognizing the benefits of capitalism, gradually began its transformation into a free-market economy.

Also during those years, the hyperinflation of the 1970s and 1980s, when double-digit inflation was the rule rather than the exception, departed, which had a dramatic impact on America's housing market. Beginning in the mid-1990s, inflation began to moderate, usually below 3 percent—often below a negligible 2 percent. This moderation in the rate of inflation had a huge impact on our nation's mortgage market. It caused a substantial reduction in the rate of interest homeowners had to pay lenders for a mortgage loan. So, instead of borrowers paying 10 percent interest or more on their mortgages, they began paying on loans at substantially reduced interest rates, at times below 5 percent.

The interest rate reductions instigated a flurry of homeowners to refinance their high-interest mortgages. In addition, and more importantly, the rate reductions gave more people the financial ability to buy a home. Some of these people were low-income renters who were now able to qualify for a mortgage loan at the lower interest rates. The lowered rates also permitted homeowners to buy additional investment property and/or to trade up to larger, more expensive homes. These investments had not been possible for many people previously because of the high interest rates of 10 percent or more. When the rates went down to 6 and then 5 percent, the monthly payments went down too, making these investments feasible. Buyers who could previously afford only a $90,000 home at 10 percent now could afford a $130,000 home at 6 percent. (The monthly principal and interest payment on a $90,000 mortgage at 10 percent for 30 years is $790, which is the same amount a borrower would pay on a $130,000 mortgage for 30 years at 6 percent.)

Low Interest Rates Raise the Demand for Real Estate

So, with lower interest rates for mortgage loans, more demand was created for homes as more people entered the home-buying market. This easing in credit conditions stimulated homeowners to not only trade up but also to begin investing in rental homes and vacation homes. Today, affluent baby boomers, rather than selling their homes as they near retirement, are buying second houses. According to the National Association of Realtors (NAR), investment homes were nearly a quarter of all purchases in 2004, and vacation homes were an additional 13 percent.

Insufficient Housing Starts and Bureaucratic Red Tape Lower the Supply

While low interest rates are raising the demand, there is pressure pushing down the supply of housing. Home builders say that, because of immigration, the present elevated level of 2 million housing starts a year is insufficient to meet higher-than-predicted growth in new households. Supply is very tight in some areas of the country because now it can take years to get new developments approved by the environmental protection agencies and the zoning authorities. The end result has been a boom in real estate values that has lasted since the late 1980s and shows no signs of dissipating.

Real Estate Boom Areas

On April 5, 2005, the Associated Press reported the following story:

Introduction

The number of areas across the United States with real estate booms grew nearly two-thirds last year to 55, the Federal Deposit Insurance Corp. said, warning that these booms may be followed by busts.

The boom areas represent 15 percent of the 362 metropolitan areas the Office of Federal Housing Enterprise Oversight [OFHEO, an agency within the U.S. Department of Housing and Urban Development] analyzes, the highest proportion of boom markets in 30 years of price data and more than twice the peak of the late-1980s booms.

Boom areas were defined as having inflation-adjusted [price increases] at the end of 2003 that were up 30 percent or more over three years.

Adding recent data and analysis to a study released in February, FDIC economists Cynthia Angell and Norman Williams repeated their view that credit market conditions may make current housing market booms different [from] past ones, which have tended to taper off rather than bust.

"To the extent that credit conditions are driving home price trends, the implication would be that a reversal in mortgage market conditions—where interest rates rise and lenders tighten their standards—could contribute to the end of the housing boom," they say.

The FDIC economists found that only 17 percent of local U.S. housing booms in the 1978–1998 period ended in busts, defined as a 15 percent or greater drop in nominal home prices over five years.

But their updated study, released May 2, 2005, also notes special qualities of the current boom, including the large number of boom markets across the country and a risky credit environment.

While the previous FDIC study on the subject in February emphasized local market factors for historical boom and bust cycles, recent past experience signals possible broader ranging causes.

"The notable expansion in the number of boom markets in 2003 suggests that national factors could be helping to drive

> home prices higher," the updated study says. "If national factors are coming more into play, then clearly the most important factors to look to would be the availability, price and terms of mortgage credit."
>
> Amid the particular risks the FDIC found in the present credit market are the greater use of adjustable-rate mortgages, expansion of interest-only payment plans, higher-leveraged new home purchases, and the acceleration in the growth of primary lenders making sub-prime loans. (*Source:* Associated Press, "Boom areas expand in U.S.," *Mississippi Sun Herald,* May 6, 2005, page C7.)

The cautiousness of the FDIC economists is shared by many real estate market observers, but there is ample reason to believe that the boom will continue unabated because of the forces of supply and demand cited in the preceding section.

The Risks of Using Adjustable-Rate Mortgages

A growing number of borrowers are choosing nontraditional financing, notably adjustable-rate mortgages (ARMs), which have interest rates that rise in tandem with market rates after a set period. Even though traditional 30-year fixed-rate loans remain below 6 percent—the lowest in decades—ARMs are being negotiated at record-setting high levels and account for more than a third of recent home lending. According to David Kogut, a senior economist at mortgage giant Fannie Mae, "Based on past experience, ARMs should have only about 20 percent of market share. The rise in ARMs reveals that borrowers are stretching to buy, because ARMs offer lower interest rates, and thus require lower monthly payments in the first year or years of a loan's term. And in the future, if market rates remain stable or fall, all these adjustable-rate loans shouldn't cause any financial problems because the associated monthly payment should stay about the same."

But what happens to these adjustable-rate mortgages when the unthinkable occurs—when market rates for mortgage loans increase; their monthly interest rate will have to be adjusted upward as will the amount of their monthly payment. Ouch! If that occurs, there will be plenty of ARM holders who will feel the crunch when they have to put the added expense of higher mortgage payments into their household budgets.

The prevalence of adjustable-rate mortgages notwithstanding, most market analysts believe that the real estate boom will continue for the foreseeable future.

(You need not worry, however, because Chapter 4, "Financing Real Estate," discusses this issue of adjustable-rate versus fixed-rate loans. In that chapter, you'll discover all the mortgage alternatives that exist so that you can make a prudent, informed decision on the type of real estate financing that best suits your particular needs.)

Why You Need Real Estate– The Classic Hedge against Uncertainty

You need real estate not only to have a place to call home but also to overcome the effects of inflation and taxes. Investing in real estate gives you a hedge against the wealth-eroding effects of inflation and income taxes. On average, you can expect your realty holdings to increase in value at least one and a half times the rate of inflation. Furthermore, in most cases, investment in real estate offers you the ability to earn tax-free rental income.

You can't make it without real estate. A big-paying job by itself likely won't make you financially independent, nor will it give you enough to retire comfortably. How do people earning average incomes gain a certain amount of financial independence? They have to invest their surplus earnings in something. What better investment vehicle than real estate. You can start with an investment in your own home. From it you not only gain a great tax write-off (mortgage interest expenses and property taxes) but over the years you also gain from the home's appreciation in value, not to mention the equity that builds up as you gradually pay down the mortgage loan. As time goes by, you can refinance and use the loan proceeds to invest in rental property.

In this day and age, you need additional income and a proven investment method to develop financial security for you and your family. Real estate investment offers you all this, and it allows you to have more control than you would have with other forms of investment. With real estate you know what your investment looks like. You can visit it. And you can keep track of the neighborhood and your rent-paying tenants.

Other forms of investment, such as common stocks, commodities, precious metals, or nonmunicipal bonds, are vulnerable to drastic price movements in unpredictable markets. Also, they do not offer the investor any form of tax shelter benefit. In contrast, real estate endures in historically stable markets. Its value may fluctuate in the short term, but over the long term, virtually every well-located property survives these up and down swings and still appreciates in value. Inflation accounts for much of this growth in value, but another contributing factor is an ever-increasing demand for housing. This is created by an ever-increasing population and real estate's unique market characteristic of limited supply—they just aren't making any more land!

Inflation and Income Taxes

In simple terms, inflation is a loss in purchasing power of the dollar. These days to survive financially, you need to protect yourself from losing money to inflation. In fact, rising consumer prices can erode your savings so much that the interest you earn on those savings will not be enough to maintain the purchasing power of the dollars you originally deposited. To make matters worse, you have to pay taxes on the earnings that accrue from the interest. This means that next year your money will be worth no more (and probably less) than it was worth this year. It will not grow. The number of dollars will increase, but they will be worth much less.

In other words, if you keep your hard-earned money in certificates of deposits (CDs) or regular savings accounts, you'll probably earn a few paltry points in interest. If you are in the 28 percent tax bracket, which most of us are, your after-tax earnings might be in the neighborhood of 1 to 2 percent. Then, if you take into account a 5 percent increase in consumer prices, your net earnings are a negative yield of about 3 to 4 percent. So if the rate of inflation averages 5 percent, for every year you keep money in a savings account, you're actually losing $3 to $4 of every $100 deposited!

Inflation and the Appreciation of Real Estate

Historically, and especially in the last 20 years, real estate has been extremely sensitive to the effects of inflation—so much so that when inflation is averaging 5 percent annually, some real estate will increase 8 to 10 percent (14 percent or more in coastal areas such as Boston, L.A., and San Francisco) during that same period. Several factors account for this appreciation of real estate. One has to do with what is called *replacement cost*. Every time a plumber, carpenter, or electrician receives a new union contract for higher wages, the cost of new residential construction goes up. And every time the cost of building supplies increases—lumber and concrete, for instance—the cost of new construction spirals upward. The result is that the house you own becomes worth about what it would cost to build it at today's prices. This is one reason why real estate in some areas has more than doubled in value during the last 10 years.

Another key factor is the limited supply of habitable land. As the land available for residential building becomes scarce, the cost of that land increases proportionately, and the increase is added into the appreciating value of your realty investment.

Other incidental factors contributing to increased realty prices are government regulations, environmental concerns with related red tape, and the increased pressure of an increasing population that demands more habitable land. As the cost of construction continues to go up, the value of new and used homes and land goes on appreciating at an even faster pace.

Here are some figures to help you fully understand how both the factors of inflation and appreciation affect you as the realty investor. Research shows that the median price for homes in the United States more than doubled in the 10 years from 1977 to 1987. In 1977 the median price—half sold for more, half sold for less—of a home was $44,000; in 1987 the price of the same home was $95,000. That's an increase of 116 percent over a decade, or an average increase of 11.6 percent annually. During that same period, the rate of inflation averaged about 5.6 percent.

More recently, according to the National Association of Realtors (NAR), during the period 2002 through 2004, the median price of single-family homes in the United States saw an average annual increase of 8.8 percent, while inflation during the same period was moderate and under 3 percent. The rate of inflation in 2002 was 1.59 percent, 2.27 percent in 2003, and 2.68 percent in 2004. In 2002 the median single-family-home price was $158,100, in 2003 it was $170,000, and in 2004 it was $184,100. Notably, in the western states the annual increase in home prices was an average of 14.1 percent with Las Vegas showing a whopping annual increase of 47.3 percent. (You should know that this substantial increase in Las Vegas is primarily due to two key factors: a tremendous growth in population there and the fact that most of the habitable land available in the Las Vegas valley, which is surrounded by mountains, has already been built on. Thus, land available for residential construction is extremely scarce.)

The Risk of Waiting

Inflation is a fact of life that has to be dealt with. Yet many people, especially those who have never owned real estate, are reluctant to invest in a home because they feel that prices are already too high, and they can't imagine that home prices will continue to escalate. These are the same people who felt that real estate was overpriced 10 years ago! So while indecisive people are sitting around grumbling about the high prices of homes, the costs of homeownership continue to rise. There will be much more to complain about tomorrow . . . . unless you act today. The house you find today, even at today's seemingly outlandish price, will cost much, much more in the future. Where real estate investment is concerned, it is never too late.

Value, Income, and the Rate of Return

Real estate investors typically look at income properties according to a simple formula:

$$V \text{ (Value)} = \frac{\text{NOI (net operating income)}}{R \text{ (rate of capitalization)}}$$

The *net operating income* (NOI) equals gross rent collections less a suitable vacancy rate and operating expenses, such as the cost of management, advertising, maintenance, repairs, insurance, and property taxes. *R* equals the rate of return the investor expects from an investment before the financing is involved. The expected rate of return, or *cap rate*, is the prevailing rate of return, which ranges between 8 and 12 percent. The actual rate applied in the financing takes into consideration the dependability of the income and the locale of the property. The lower rates represent better-quality neighborhoods and more reliable tenants. (For more details on cap rates, see Chapter 7, "Appraisals.")

Here's how the numbers work given an NOI of $18,000 and an expected rate of return of 10 percent before the consideration of financing:

$$V \text{ (value, or selling price)} = \frac{\$18{,}000 \text{ (NOI)}}{0.10\ (R)} = \$180{,}000$$

Investors typically choose a lower rate of return when they feel they have good reasons to expect high rates of appreciation on a particular property. For instance, in southern California and parts of northern California, particularly Marin County, you often see cap rates (*R*) of 6 percent or less. Notice the value-increasing effects you have in low-yield real estate markets when cap rates are reduced from an average of 8 percent down to 5 percent:

$$\frac{\$18{,}000 \text{ (NOI)}}{0.08\ (R)} = \$225{,}000\ (V)$$

$$\frac{\$18{,}000 \text{ (NOI)}}{0.07\ (R)} = \$257{,}143\ (V)$$

$$\frac{\$18{,}000 \text{ (NOI)}}{0.06\ (R)} = \$300{,}000\ (V)$$

$$\frac{\$18{,}000 \text{ (NOI)}}{0.05\ (R)} = \$360{,}000\ (V)$$

Appreciation Plus Increased Rents

Besides the benefit of appreciation, you also gain as the growing population bids up rents as they compete for a limited supply of housing to acquire a home of their own. Say you purchase a four-unit rental property today for $160,000. Six years later rents have increased from $16,000 to $20,000. The cap rate (*R*) has fallen from 10 percent to 8 percent. So the property you purchased six years ago has increased in value by $90,000 to $250,000:

$$\frac{\$20{,}000\ (\text{NOI})}{0.08\ (R)} = \$250{,}000\ (V)$$

Black Monday

Certain stock market events, such as "Black Monday"—October 19, 1987—when the market crashed 508 points in one frantic session, serve to emphasize the enduring value of owning a home. Most Americans prefer safe investments with historically good performance records. Homeownership is one of those standards of enduring value, and as a result, American consumers have most of their wealth invested in the homes in which they live. They have made this choice because investment in a home gives them a hedge against inflation and an opportunity to accumulate wealth for the future. And homeownership provides other wonderful benefits too.

Benefits of Owning versus Renting a Home

Compare two similar families: Each family is made up of two income-earning adults and one dependent child, and each family has a combined gross income of $40,000. Each family has $10,000 to invest. One family buys a $100,000 home, investing $10,000 in the down payment and creating a $90,000 first mortgage at 6 percent fixed interest for 30 years. The other family continues to rent a home at $950 a month and invests its $10,000 in a CD that earns 3 percent annual interest.

Assume that the family incomes, rents, and the value of the purchased home increase 8 percent a year and that inflation rises 3 percent. At the end of the first year, the homeowner family pays $1,505 less in federal income taxes because the interest on the mortgage is tax deductible, the value of their home will have increased by $8,000, and they will have built up $1,104 in equity by paying down the mortgage. The renter family will see a $300 gain on their CD at the end of the first year.

At the end of five years, the homeowners will have paid about $7,190 less in federal income taxes, and their home will be worth $146,910, for a gain of $46,910. Were the homeowners to sell their home and buy

Figure I.1 Advantages of Owning versus Renting a Home

	Tax Deduction	Gain in Value	Equity Buildup	Taxes on Gain
		After First Year		
Homeowner	$1,505	$8,000	$1,104	Deferred
Renter (CD)	0	300	0	$84
		After Five Years		
Homeowner	$7,190	$46,910	$6,021	Deferred
Renter (CD)	0	1,593	0	446

another of greater value, they could defer paying income tax on the gain from the first house. Or, if they simply sold it, they would not have to pay taxes until they reached $500,000 in capital gains. In contrast, the renter's $10,000 CD would be worth $11,593 after five years, for a gain of $1,593, which would be taxable.

Figure I.1 illustrates the tremendous gains that can be achieved through homeownership in comparison to home rental. Note especially the equity buildup column, which reveals the homeowner's growing share of equity in the home as the mortgage is paid down.

From this illustration, which considers the three factors of tax deductibility, appreciation in value, and equity buildup, we can see that the homeowner's net gain after five years is $58,974. That gain is clearly much greater than the renters' net gain from their $10,000 CD. So here we have a clear case in favor of homeownership.

Other Benefits of Investing in Real Estate

Besides the advantages of beating inflation and gaining steady appreciation, there are many other benefits of owning real estate and reasons it will outperform other traditional investments:

- You have personal control.
- You don't need much to get started.
- You get forced savings from the principal buildup benefit.
- You earn tax benefits.
- It's easy to learn the how-tos of profitable realty investing.

You Have Personal Control

Owning a home or other income-producing realty not only gives you a wonderful feeling of pride in yourself. It also gives you confidence because it is a tangible asset. You can see it, feel it, and improve on it. Furthermore, you can usually rest assured that your real estate investment will likely increase in value because real estate in general has appreciated consistently for hundreds of years. Granted, values can become depressed in the short term, but over the long haul almost every well-located improved property will appreciate in value. And most important, you'll have personal control over your realty investments in historically stable markets. In contrast, most other investment opportunities occur in very unpredictable markets.

Simply stated, there's virtually no better investment available—none that give you total control, none that exist in a market that traditionally appreciates, and none that give you as great a hedge against inflation. And at this point I want to emphasize the phrase *total control* because there's an important lesson here. Unlike investing in stocks or bonds, with real estate you don't have to rely on third-party agents to handle or manipulate your hard-earned investment money. That's because *you* make the critical decision as to what to invest in. Granted, you may heed the advice of knowledgeable Realtors or friends, but it's you who will ultimately either live in the investment and care for it or decide who rents it. And it's you who will thereby have command of its usage.

You Don't Need Much to Get Started

A few thousand dollars is all most people need to get started with buying a home, and under certain circumstances some people don't even need that. This book reveals several highly leveraged financing techniques (see Chapter 2, "Profitable Investment Strategies"). For instance, if you're a qualified veteran, you can borrow up to $203,000 with no money down. Or if you qualify under an insured FHA (Federal Housing Administration) loan, you can borrow up to $208,000 with just 3 percent for a down payment. (Chapter 4 shows you several low-cost methods to finance real estate, some with no money down.)

In the financial world, *leverage* is the use of a small amount of cash to control a much greater amount of assets. "Zero leverage" would be a full-cash purchase; a purchase "90 percent leveraged" would combine a 10 percent down payment with 90 percent financing. Because of the impact of steady appreciation and inflation on real estate values, you can achieve the greatest yield on your invested dollars by getting as much leverage as possible when purchasing real estate.

For another example of leverage, consider the purchase of a home using 95 percent leverage (borrowing 95 percent of the purchase price along with a 5 percent down payment), as opposed to purchasing the same property with zero leverage (a full-cash purchase with no financing). Using these terms, suppose you bought a house for $100,000 with a $5,000 down payment (5 percent). A year later you realize an $8,000 increase in the value of the home, which makes the house now worth $108,000. Because you put only $5,000 down on the house and it appreciated $8,000, you have realized a 160 percent return on your investment ($8,000 return divided by $5,000 invested).

Now, using different terms, suppose you purchase the same house for $100,000 cash (zero leverage), and a year later, as it happened in the previous example, the value of that property has increased to $108,000. In this case, your investment is $100,000, the appreciation is still $8,000, but the return (yield) is only 8 percent on the investment ($8,000 divided by $100,000).

Unlike buying common stock on the New York Stock Exchange, you can purchase a $100,000 home with as little as $3,000 for a down payment (or nothing down if you're a qualified veteran). To make your first purchase of $100,000 of common stock, you have to come up with at least $50,000 in cash (50 percent). And if the stock you purchase declines in value, you'll unfortunately get a margin call requiring that you add cash to the account. If you do not meet the stockbroker's margin requirements, the stock could be liquidated to satisfy the deficit, and you'll be stuck with the loss. But there are no margin calls in real estate. Even in the unlikely event that your home declines in value your mortgage lender cannot require you to invest more cash into the home just to maintain a specified loan-to-value ratio.

Moreover, not only can you invest in real estate with far less cash than you would need to invest in an equivalent amount of stock, but financing real estate is not nearly as risky, and it's much less complicated than using leveraged margin accounts to buy stocks. Using margin accounts to invest in a volatile, unpredictable stock market is a risky game played mostly by brave speculators.

You Get Forced Savings from the Principal Build-Up Benefit

Figure I.2 shows what happens to a $10,000 down payment on a $110,000 home over 30 years based on conservative appreciation rates of just 3, 5, and 7 percent. Note that based on only a 3 percent appreciation rate, as the loan pays down over 30 years, the homeowner can expect his or her value to grow to $270,160 from an initial down payment of $10,000. At 5 percent, he or she can expect a $10,000 down payment to increase to $491,370 in 30 years. And at 7 percent, a similar down payment would grow to $892,760 by year 30.

You can see from Figure I.2 that over an extended period a beginning equity of $10,000 can grow significantly—from both the factors of appreciation and mortgage pay-down—into hundreds of thousands of dollars. Better yet, if you improve your property and invest in a hot real estate market (properties in the western United States have appreciated at 14.1 percent annually for the last four years), you can pyramid your wealth by trading up to larger properties that much faster. (See Chapter 11, "How to Retire on Your Realty Investments.")

Typically, when you own a home for many years, it becomes an integral part of your financial net worth. Over the long haul you will be making financial gains from the appreciation in the value of your home as well as from the equity that will build up as you pay down the mortgage. *Home equity* is the difference between the home's market value and the outstanding mortgage balance, and it can develop into hundreds of thousands of dollars that you can benefit from in several ways. For example, you can refinance your home and live off your earned equity. Or you can sell the home and finance the buyer's mortgage yourself so that you will receive the interest-bearing installment payments and you can do whatever you want with them. Your home can even be a great source of retirement income. (See Chapter 11, "How to Retire on Your Realty Investments.")

Figure I.2 Building Wealth with Appreciation and Equity Buildup

Appreciation	Year 0		Year 10		Year 20		Year 30	
3% rate	Value	$110,000	Value	$148,380	Value	$200,170	Value	$270,150
	Loan	100,000	Loan	86,790	Loan	58,900	Loan	0
	Equity	10,000	Equity	61,590	Equty	141,270	Equity	270,150
5% rate	Value	110,000	Value	181,380	Value	298,300	Value	491,300
	Loan	100,000	Loan	86,780	Loan	58,900	Loan	0
	Equity	10,000	Equity	94,600	Equity	239,400	Equity	491,300
7% rate	Value	110,000	Value	220,900	Value	444,100	Value	892,700
	Loan	100,000	Loan	86,790	Loan	58,900	Loan	0
	Equity	10,000	Equity	134,110	Equity	385,200	Equity	892,700

You Earn Tax Benefits

Keep in mind that the income tax law favors homeowners and realty investors. As a renter, you get absolutely no tax relief. But as a homeowner, the loan origination points, mortgage interest, and property taxes you pay are deductible against your federal, state, and local income taxes. Also, compared to the fully taxable dividends you receive from stock ownership, when you sell your home, the capital gain of up to $500,000 is exempt from income taxes. And *active* income property owners are allowed to shelter some of their rental income from federal, state, and local income taxes. (See the discussion of "active" and "passive" tax laws in Chapter 12, "How to Avoid Paying Too Much in Taxes.")

Note also that if you sell a winning stock intending to move the proceeds into another stock or a managed fund, you'll be required to pay a good portion of your gain to the IRS. With an individual retirement account (IRA), 401(k), or other tax-sheltered retirement plan, you may defer some of the taxes on the gains; yet many regulations and restrictions apply to these plans. However, you avoid these kinds of income taxes in real estate, which means you get to keep your entire accumulated wealth as long as you own properties. In addition, through home equity loans, refinancing, or installment sales, you can extract cash out of your realty holdings with little or no payment of income taxes.

It's Easy to Learn the How-Tos of Profitable Realty Investing

Satisfied home buyers and successful income property investors didn't get that way by recklessly throwing their money around, making ill-advised decisions such as paying too much for the wrong type of financing or overbuying a poorly located property in a declining neighborhood. To the contrary, they made educated, informed decisions based on well-defined guidelines.

To be successful at realty investing, you're not going to need a real estate license or a college degree. You don't even need experience. What you do need is perseverance, commitment, and a willingness to learn and apply the lessons given in the following chapters. That, along with a good knowledge of your local area and property values, will take you a long way toward achieving your real estate investment goals.

Benefits of Owning Rental Property

Besides the benefits of appreciation, equity buildup, and tax write-offs for homeowners, there's more good news for rental property owners.

Dependability of Rental Income

Yes, you might be saying, "You convinced me that rental property is a great investment. But what about vacancies and troublesome tenants who don't pay their rent? Who needs that kind of nightmare?"

Good questions. That's the reason Chapter 10 shows you how to efficiently optimize profits using proven hassle-free methods to manage your property. When you follow the guidelines and policies discussed later in the book, you learn how to attract good tenants, supervise your resident managers, and make your property more desired.

What the Future Holds for Rental Property

Overall, the future appears very bright. You can expect increasing rents and appreciation. Although short-term recessions may temporarily cause an increase in vacancies and depress rents, rent levels and appreciation will rise over the long term. Essentially, this will be caused by the future demand for rental real estate that will increase faster than future supply. Here are four reasons why:

1. *Growth in U.S. population.* Using conservative growth expectations, the U.S. population over the next 20 years, primarily from immigration, is expected to increase from its current figure of 287 million to 337 million—an increase of 50 million people. So, in just two decades, the United States will add more people than are currently living in the three states of Florida, Michigan, and Texas.
2. *Growth in the number of U.S. households.* Americans currently average 2.2 persons per household, but that number has recently been declining. It will likely decrease to about 2.0, given the latest trends of families having fewer children, more singles living alone, and more baby boomers born in the 1940s phasing into retirement. Then America will require 25 million additional housing units just

to adequately house the 50 million people that will be added to the population.

3. *Growth in personal income.* People need money to buy houses or rent a home. Accordingly, people earn more money when unemployment is low and general economic conditions are strong. So what does the future hold for growth in the U.S. economy? Will it be productive, and can it adequately supply the employment required to produce this income? You would be pleased to know that the outlook for growth in the U.S. economy is very optimistic. Expansion of worldwide markets for U.S. products due to globalization, increased levels of competition among businesses, and technical innovation will lead to increased incomes and economic productivity. Moreover, a growing number of two-earner households substantially raises the overall household disposable income.
4. *Growth in second-home ownership.* As of this writing more that 8 million American households own a second home. Considering the present market conditions that encourage more real estate investment—a growth in population of 50 million more people who need housing, low interest rates for mortgage loans, and dispirited stock investors bailing out of unpredictable markets to invest in real estate—economists predict this number to increase significantly over the next 20 years. They're forecasting that by 2025 more than 20 million households will own at least two homes.

Twenty years of growing population, as you can see, will result in record numbers of people needing adequate housing. There's even more good news for realty investors and that has to do with interest rates.

Inflation and the Nominal Mortgage Rate

The rate of interest mortgage lenders charge borrowers can have a dramatic affect on real estate markets. Low interest rates encourage demand for real estate; conversely, higher interest rates inhibit demand.

When interest rates are low, real estate values generally appreciate at a faster pace because more people can qualify for a mortgage at 6

Figure I.3 History of Nominal Mortgage Rates and Inflation (*Source*: U.S. Department of Labor.)

Year	Nominal Rate	CPI Increase	Real Rate
1950	4.5	1.3	3.2
1960	5.0	1.7	3.3
1970	8.56	5.7	2.86
1980	13.95	13.5	.45
1990	10.08	5.4	4.68
2002	6.5	1.6	4.9
2003	5.58	2.3	3.28
2004	5.7	2.7	3.0
2005	5.9 (est)	3.4 (est)	2.5 (est)

percent than could at 9 or 10 percent. For instance, using the FHA standard of a home buyer's ability to pay 29 percent of his or her gross monthly income for a mortgage payment, a wage earner who makes $25,000 annually could afford a monthly payment of principal and interest (*P* and *I*) of $604. At a 10 percent rate of interest over 30 years, that wage earner could afford to borrow only $70,000. But at 6 percent, the same wage earner could afford to qualify for a $100,000 mortgage, keeping his or her monthly *P* and *I* at about the same $604.

Note in Figure I.3 that during the 1980s, nominal mortgage rates and inflation were at their highest levels, but the real rate was at its lowest. [Economists use the term *real rate of interest* to mean the difference between the nominal mortgage interest rate and the annual increase in the consumer price index (CPI).]

Is Real Estate Right for You?

Although owning a home or lots of rental property can be profitable and fun, these things do not happen without a certain amount of work and effort on your part. I have prepared for you a complete guide to buying and managing real estate without all the ordinary hassles most landlords endure. It is you, however, who must implement the guidelines given. You must locate the right property to invest in, negotiate with the seller for its purchase, locate quality tenants, collect rents, and handle improvements and repair.

Only you can determine whether you're capable of performing these functions. They are the drawbacks of owning income-producing real estate. Now consider the advantages: Improved real estate, on average, will appreciate more than one and a half times the rate of inflation. That's at least 1.5 times the increase in the cost of living, and it will give you a great hedge against inflation.

Owning a home is best if you intend to stay put for a while. If you plan to relocate out of state within three years of your buying the home, then owning a home is usually not practical. The acquisition costs with the usual incidentals, not to mention the costs to renovate and sell, are hard to overcome in the short term. Remember, real estate is always better as a long-term investment.

Not only, then, is inflation on your side as a realty owner, so is time. As time passes, rents can be increased, while most of your operating expenses, such as your fixed-rate mortgage, remain the same. This means that the property you initially purchased, which had little or no cash flow then, can in time develop positive cash flow from annual rental increases.

Many property owners who have been fortunate enough to hold on to their properties for the long haul are eventually able to virtually live off the earned rental income. In other words, income property purchased today with a minimal down payment is unlikely to net a positive cash flow. But, as time passes, the property appreciates and the rents are gradually increased, and over the long term, these will produce more and more income for the owner. Therefore, the longer you own the property, the greater the net income from it becomes. Furthermore, during the time of ownership, you enjoy the tax shelter benefits from the property. In other words, *buy all the income property you can when you're young, then enjoy the income benefits when you're older.*

Besides the benefits of appreciation, increasing income, and tax shelter, you also have a tremendous refinancing benefit. You can periodically refinance your realty holdings as the mortgage loan balances diminish and your equity position becomes substantial. Every 5 or 10 years, you can refinance certain properties, pulling out cash to reinvest in more properties or doing whatever you want with it.

Still another method of income production can be created when the owner of real estate decides to sell. After you have owned property for an extended period, you will, more than likely, realize a sizable capital gain from the sale. You have the options of taking all cash from the gain or of accepting an interest-bearing note for your equity in the property. (As of this writing, the IRS allows an individual taxpayer who owns a home and lives in it for two out of the last five years prior to the sale to completely avoid taxes on up to $250,000 in capital gains. Married taxpayers filing jointly can exclude up to $500,000 in gains.)

Where Will You Be?

Variations on how real estate can provide income for its owner are virtually boundless. But where will you as an individual be as time goes on? That's entirely up to you. You can either be a renter or a homeowner and/or landlord. As a renter, you're only a tiny cog in the great financial wheels of progress as you continue to pay rent (which is income to the landlord) just to have a roof over your head. Or you can join in the general prosperity that's enjoyed by the deserving and elite class of people who are homeowners and landlords. If you become knowledgeable and experienced about real estate, you can use this knowledge and, with careful planning, take control of your own future. Even if all you do is purchase a home for you and your family, you have the privilege at the end of the day to return to your appreciating investment . . . to that wonderful parcel of earth that belongs solely to you and that has often been called "home, sweet home."

1

Rules for Successful Real Estate Investing

Key Points

- *Setting your goals*
- *Achieving your goals*
- *Learning to specialize*
- *Staying with what you know*
- *Learning as much as you can about your local realty market*
- *Looking at real estate as a long-term investment*

If you have the ambition to someday be a successful realty investor and want to optimize your profits along the way, then I offer you a set of success-oriented rules for consideration. Keep in mind, though, that Rome wasn't built in a day and your fortune in real estate holdings won't be either. You need time. But more than that, you need a specific plan that spells out how you will reach your goals regardless of whether they're related to buying a home just for you and your family or buying a vast multitude of income-producing properties you can retire on. If you want financial independence through investment in real estate, then you need a well-conceived plan to achieve that goal. First, you need to set realistic goals and the steps you need to take to achieve them. Next you have to learn how to specialize in specific types of real estate. You also have to stay with what you know or with what you do best, and you have to learn as much as you can about the local realty market.

Setting Your Goals

An inspirational Chinese proverb that has been passed on over the years from our parents or peers goes like this: "A journey of a thousand miles begins with a single step." Your journey can begin by setting certain goals, and then using the established guidelines that are presented throughout this book to achieve them.

Goal 1. Establish Your Credit and Make Wise Use of It

For beginners to realty investing, goal 1 is linked to an old axiom that says, "Before you can run, you must first learn how to walk!" In real estate investing, that means if you want to borrow money from primary lenders, you need to first make sure your credit is established. (Those of you who already have borrowed to invest in real estate and have established credit can skip over goal 1.)

You have to have good credit so you can borrow the needed money to make real estate investments. If you've never had credit before, now is the time to establish it. Start with a consumer credit card or open an account with a major retailer, and develop a credit history.

The Wise Use of Credit

Frivolous spending with consumer credit cards while incurring monthly interest charges on the unpaid balance and not being capable of paying it off every month can get you in serious financial trouble. But, on the other hand, when you borrow money to invest in real estate, you are using credit wisely. This is true especially when you are borrowing money to purchase income property because you're using rental income to pay down the debt. You're, in effect, a partner with the lender on the property, but you don't have to pay your partner a share of the profits. Instead, you only have to pay them interest on the money borrowed.

Goal 2. Decide What You Are Going to Buy

Your second goal could be to purchase your first home. Or, if you already own a home, your goal could be to invest in a second home to fix up and reside in and find a rent-paying tenant for the home you moved from. Part of this goal is to decide on precisely what you're going to buy—for example, a detached single-family residence for you or your family. (Buying a detached single-family residence is a key guideline to making a superior realty investment. It, along with 10 other key guidelines, are detailed in Chapter 3.)

If you already own your own home and live in it, the reason I recommend renting it out and moving in to the new investment is because it's more efficient. It is easier to rent out the property you are already in because potential renters would come to you instead of your driving to the property to meet them. And later it will be easier to renovate the new acquisition if you're already living in it instead of constantly driving back and forth to it from your home.

Goal 3. Determine Your Borrowing Capacity

Determine your borrowing capacity because that amount, along with the down payment, is the maximum price you can afford. For now, that amount is about three times your gross income. So if you earn $40,000 a year, you can qualify to borrow up to $120,000. (For more details about how much you can borrow, see Chapter 4, "Financing Real Estate.")

Goal 4. Save for the Down Payment

Start saving some of your money for the down payment if you haven't already saved it. In determining how much money you need to save to meet your investment goals, keep in mind that you don't need that much money for a down payment. In fact, if you're a qualified veteran you can borrow up to $203,000 with nothing down. And under FHA requirements, all you need is 3 percent of the purchase price, which is only $3,600 on a $120,000 home. (Again, see Chapter 4 for more details on financing real estate purchases.)

The key to saving money is to get control of your spending, which you can accomplish in the following ways:

- *Reward yourself first.* Don't think "budget"—it sounds too much like work. Instead, think "reward." If you are a renter, consider the wonderful reward you can earn for yourself and your family by allocating your money toward a beautiful home of your own. If a new home is truly what you want, stop spending on nonessentials and begin allocating that money toward a down payment.

  To stop overspending, Robert Maurer, psychologist and author of the book *How One Small Step Can Change Your Life: The Kaizen Way* (Workman Publishing, New York, $16.95), says to remove one object from the shopping cart before heading to the cash register. In his book, Maurer writes that once he decided to lose weight, he didn't avoid all carbohydrates or hire a pricey personal weight trainer. Instead, he decided to throw out the first French fry on his plate. Eventually, it became two, then three French fries, or a tiny bit of whatever other food he was eating. In this way, Maurer lost 45 pounds in 18 months and became a living example of the premise of his book.
- *Chop up those credit cards.* Stop charging on the credit cards now and make a commitment to start living within your established means (net income). If you think you may have a problem doing this, consider chopping up the credit cards so you can't use them. Put yourself on a strictly cash diet. Nothing curbs frivolous spending better than paying in hard cash. Besides, you can always reapply for other cards once the balances are paid off. A credit card can be a very useful buying tool if properly utilized—when you maintain a zero balance by making charges and paying off the balance when it's due. This way you don't incur interest and carrying charges.

  If you already own your home and have a sizable amount of equity in it, consider taking out a low-interest home-equity loan, which *is* tax deductible, and using the proceeds to pay off all that credit-card debt, which is *not* tax deductible.
- *Reduce your housing expense.* Rent is the biggest expense for most people who do not own their home. You can reduce the cost of rent by taking the following measures: Switch to a lower-cost apart-

ment or share a rental—for example, you and two friends could share a three-bedroom house or apartment, or you could rent an empty bedroom to someone, or you could move in with your parents or relatives and be rent free for six months. These measures may sound drastic, but imagine a savings of $750 a month for half a year. That's a total savings of $4,500. Make that your down payment on a home, and you'll never pay rent again!

- *Rid yourself of that extra car, or downsize the one you drive.* If you have an extra vehicle and you can do without it, by all means sell it. This way you rid yourself of all the extra costs, such as the monthly loan payments, maintenance, fuel, licensing, and insurance. In particular, you should get rid of the cash-draining car payments. If the old car is almost paid off and you're considering buying or leasing a new one, don't! Drive the most dependable least expensive automobile you can find. Car payments—in particular, monthly lease payments—are the bane of far too many renters, and they will most certainly inhibit most saving plans.

Achieving Your Goals

Start with the purchase of a single-family home if you don't already own your home. If your long-term goal is to get rich and retire on your real estate, that's fine. That's a long-term goal. But first you need a short-term goal to get you to your long-term goal. You need to buy that first property before you can have several properties. So your initial goal is to buy a home for you and your family. And if your current credit status in not worthy of getting a mortgage, then your first goal will be to get your credit up to date. That's your first priority. Then you can make buying your home your second goal.

Single-family residences are great investments. They're always in demand because they're the type of home most people—both renters and home buyers alike—prefer to live in. You could learn to specialize by investing in them. Generally, you should avoid investing in any kind of attached housing, such as condominiums and co-operative apartments. There are several reasons why: First, there's not as much demand for them as there is for other types of properties, so they don't appreciate in value as

Landlord Tale

In 1971, when I was a senior at Michigan State University, my grandmother passed away, and I inherited from her $10,000 and a house full of furniture. Within six months, through aggressive margin buying and ill-advised stock tips, I managed to whittle down my inheritance to $5,000. It was then that one of my professors, Gene Dunham, advised me to use the remaining cash to buy a house near the university. He said it would not only preserve what I had left but it would help me save on storage fees and be a great place to keep the inherited furniture.

So I took his advice and purchased a nice little home in Lansing, moved the furniture in, and rented it to three MSU students. But I still had $1,500 left over, and I thought how nice it would be to have a second house, especially one I could live in. Soon I found a great prospect. It was a huge six-bedroom home situated on a half-acre of land on the outskirts of the campus. The problem was, in order to assume the existing low-interest loan, I would have to come up with an $8,500 down payment, which left me $7,000 short.

It was at about this time that I discovered the Federal Housing Administration (FHA) and all the great financing programs it has to offer both homeowners and potential homeowners. Under Title II, the FHA has an insured-loan program to assist in the financing and renovation of an owner-occupied home. Since I would be occupying the property and intended to remodel it, a Title II loan would be ideal. At the time I also had three credit cards at my disposal, with a combined line of credit that would cover the $7,000, which, along with my $1,500, was what I needed for the down payment.

So from the three credit cards, I borrowed the $7,000 and purchased the home. Then, with the help of FHA, I took out a renovation loan for $7,000 amortized for five years and used the proceeds to pay off the $7,000 debt incurred on the credit cards.

After all was said and done, I moved into this beauty and rented out the other five bedrooms to MSU students. Remarkably, after paying on both loans and along with property taxes and insurance, I lived in this home for free and still had a $150 a month profit.

Note that primary lenders usually frown on borrowing the down payment for a mortgage loan. But in the preceding situation, since the first mortgage was assumed and did not require qualification, there was no concern about the source of the down payment.

much as detached single-family dwellings. Co-ops, in particular, because of the way the individual units are titled, can be difficult to finance and sell. And with both condos and co-ops, you're stuck with association fees that are always increasing. (For more information, see Chapter 3, "Key Guidelines for Making a Superior Realty Investment.")

After you have some experience at investing you can make other types of realty investments, such as 2- to 4-unit apartment buildings. Then you can tackle even bigger residential rentals, such as 20-unit or larger apartment buildings.

Learning to Specialize and Stay with What You Know or with What You Do Best

Physicians specialize in a certain field of medicine in order to gain expertise. So do attorneys; this is how they become experts in their field of endeavor. It's difficult to become very knowledgeable in a wide range of subjects, especially in such broad professions as medicine and law. This is why most professional people specialize.

Donald Trump's experience with the commercial airline business is a prime example of why you should stay with what you do best—because the minute you get into a field you're not familiar with, it's easy to take a fall. After making billions successfully developing much of Manhattan's prime real estate, in 1989, in the midst of a prolonged aircraft mechanic's strike, Trump decided to buy the Eastern Shuttle, which was originally part of the now-defunct Eastern Airlines. Financed through a syndicate of 22 banks with a $380 million loan, Trump Air began on June 7 with hourly flights of Boeing 727 aircraft from New York's LaGuardia Airport to Boston's Logan International Airport and Washington's National Airport in Arlington, Virginia.

Trump pushed to make the new shuttle a luxury air service and a marketing vehicle for the Trump name. Its aircraft were decorated with features such as maple wood veneer, gold lavatory fixtures, and chrome seat-belt latches. Trump Air also made advancements in certain technologies; it introduced the first passenger self-service kiosks at its LaGuardia base, and it offered rented laptop computers to passengers.

Almost from its inception, Trump Air encountered financial problems. The shuttle's core passengers chose it for its convenience, not for its costly luxury features, and during the prolonged labor strike, many defected to the competing Pan Am Shuttle or to Amtrak's Metroliner service. To make matters worse, in 1989 the northeast states entered an economic recession that depressed demand, and the August 1990 Iraqi invasion of Kuwait caused jet fuel prices to double.

The Trump Shuttle never turned a profit. The overextended debt load incurred in the company's formation unnerved Trump's creditors as his other high-profile, highly leveraged interests showed signs of failing. In September 1990 the loans were defaulted, and the creditor banks took over ownership of the airline.

George Ross, lead author of *Trump Strategies for Real Estate* (Wiley, 2005) and Trump's executive and legal advisor, said that part of the reason Trump Air got into financial trouble was the lender's exuberance to lend Trump money. Up until the experience with Trump Air, everything Trump touched turned into gold; therefore, lenders were more than willing to lend him money for just about anything he wanted to do, even if the enterprise wasn't within his field of expertise.

So, instead of attempting to be knowledgeable in many types of real estate business, specialize and do what you do best. That way you will become very competent and knowledgeable in your own field.

Learning As Much As You Can about Your Local Real Estate Market

When you become familiar with a particular area, you gain knowledge. Knowledge becomes power that you can use to make better deals because you become an informed investor. You eventually become more efficient because you don't need to research—you already know the answer. When you know values such as replacement costs per square foot, rental rates, the value of building lots, it's easier to spot a bargain or to quickly determine whether a property deserves further attention. Also, if you know what it costs to make certain improvements, or if you have knowledge about certain changes coming to a particular area, such as new roads or major shopping centers, you can capitalize on the coming changes.

Looking at Real Estate As a Long-Term Investment

Residential real estate is a better long-term investment than a short-term one. Over the long haul, you'll make more money holding on to your real estate investments than you will "flipping" them (selling them quickly). Here are several reasons why:

- After the sale you'll have to find another property to invest the proceeds in; otherwise you might be tempted to squander the gains.
- Under certain circumstances, you'll be required to pay taxes on the gain. Obviously there would be no tax liability if you didn't sell.
- The costs of procuring a sale can eat up your profits. Perpetual sales, especially when you have to pay a realtor's sales commission, can get very costly.
- Often when you invest in real estate with a small down payment and then rent it out, in the first year or two it's difficult to earn a great return. Often you will just break even or have a short period of a little negative cash flow. But as time passes, you'll have the opportunity to increase rents and earn a much better return.
- And most important, you'll enjoy the benefit of growing equity through years of appreciation and mortgage pay-down, which would be missing in a short-term sale.

Chapter Lessons

- You may not like the idea of living with a group of people in a share-rental situation, but if it means that you can someday acquire a certain level of financial independence by owning a lot of income property, then it's probably worth it!
- Credit cards are only useful if they're properly used. Overspending on nonessentials with consumer debt, especially when the debt incurs interest and is not paid off each month, is not conducive to living within your means. Mortgage debt, however, is necessary in your overall strategy to acquire real estate, in particular, income-producing real estate. This is true because the mortgage debt you incur produces income that can be used to pay off the mortgage debt.
- To build up your savings, curb your expenses and pay yourself first.
- Specialization is the key to becoming knowledgeable and efficient at real estate investing. Being a so-called Jack of all trades is okay, but when you specialize in something, you will develop solid expertise in it.
- Owning rental property over the long term is, in most cases, more profitable and efficient than constantly buying and selling real estate over short-term periods. This is because over the long term, your costs will remain relatively stable while rents will always be increasing. In contrast, if you sell your real estate after owning it for just a short time, you not only have to pay taxes on the earned gains but you also have to invest in another property rather quickly so that you don't squander your gains. And you can feel confident in keeping properties over the long haul. Land has supreme value because of its finite supply. In other words, they're just not making any more of it. And for that reason alone, land that's well located will always be in demand and will always increase in value. Experienced, savvy realty investors such as Donald Trump, never sell their holdings outright because they know if they do, they will have to pay taxes on the gain. They also know that they will have to reinvest the proceeds quickly, and they know how difficult it is to find another profitable investment. That's why they maintain a long-term strategy of buy and hold for their real estate investments.

2

Profitable Investment Strategies

How to Earn Great Returns on a Modest Investment

Key Points

- *Utilizing the profitable strategies of renting to tenants, renting and giving a buy-option, land banking, and making conversions*
- *Writing a business plan before you buy*

The Investment Strategies

There are several alternative holding strategies to consider before you purchase a particular property. You could, for example, simply rent the property to a tenant; or you could do even better and give the tenant an option to buy it, which earns additional income through option fees. There's also the alternative of holding the property with the intention of later changing it to a higher use (called *land banking*). You could perhaps convert apartment units to condominiums or convert a house to office space. And you have the alternative strategy of *fix and flip*, which is investing in fixer-uppers and quickly selling for a profit. Once you've thought about these strategies, you can direct your energy to the strategy that will best suit your needs, ability, and long-term goals.

Renting to Tenants

After you've owned your home for a while and feel it's time to invest in another property, you could find another house to purchase for your primary residence and rent out the home you now live in. This strategy is efficient because you can direct tenant applicants to meet you at your home, instead of your having to drive to the rental to show it every time an interested applicant wants to see the property.

Renting Out Part of Your Home

The objective with this strategy is to purchase a larger house than you actually need, make part of it your residence, and make the other part a rental unit. For instance, purchase a large two-story home with, say, 1,500 square feet upstairs and similar square footage downstairs. The rental unit should have a separate entrance, with a kitchen, at least one bathroom, and a bedroom or two. This way the tenant has less opportunity to be a nuisance by using your entrance and kitchen.

This type of rental arrangement has several benefits. Under federal tax law you can depreciate part of your residence (the rental unit) and deduct it against rental income. You also have the benefit of having someone to look after your property when you're away, and perhaps feed the dog and gather your mail.

Renting to College Students

If you live in a college town, consider buying a big house with lots of bedrooms, then converting it into a boarding house and renting out the bedrooms to several college students. The larger bedrooms could accommodate two students, while others would pay more for their private rooms.

Location is crucial for student housing. If the property is near the campus, you can accommodate students willing to walk or ride a bike to class. If your potential boarding house is situated more than a few miles from campus, you're restricted to tenants who have a motorized vehicle.

Landlord Tale

In December 2004, my wife Jenny and I purchased a 2,200-square-foot ranch-style home on a beautiful piece of property not far from the Gulf Coast of southern Mississippi. Although it was only two miles from the interstate, it was away from all the urban tract housing, situated in a quiet country setting among beautiful rolling hills on 3.2 acres, with a 1,600-square-foot cabinet shop nearby. And it was the cabinet shop that gave this property its potential as a great moneymaker because I could easily convert it to a rentable guest house. It had adequate size, it was sturdy, it was built on a concrete slab, and it had four solid insulated walls with adequate windows. There were, however, several problems to overcome. The shop only had 40 amps of power, which came from the main house. And it did not have water, heat, air-conditioning, or any plumbing whatsoever.

Instead of designing it with lots of rooms, we decided to go with a spacious, open design and made it into a large two-bedroom one-bath house. We textured all the walls and ceilings, installed first-rate equipment throughout, including central heating and air, along with remote-controlled ceiling fans, and we finished off the floors with a combination of thick Berber carpeting and ceramic tile. When all was said and done, and after hiring three craftsmen to help me build it, and with three months of hard work and total expenditures of about $18,000, the guest rental house was finally complete. It turned out beautifully; and three weeks later we had it rented for $895 a month.

Now I have two finished houses on the property where once there was only a house and an old cabinet shop. And the property is worth in excess of $300,000—an increase in value of $110,000—while I invested only $18,000 to create that added value.

You, of course, would have to furnish it, and you would have to require substantial deposits to cover potential damage.

Choosing between Short- and Long-Term Agreements

Renting houses or apartments has always been a great way for realty investors to show a good return on their investment. On a basic rental, you have to decide whether to use a long-term lease or a month-to-month rental agreement. The long-term lease of one year or more has one essential advantage, that of securing a tenant and limiting tenant turnover and somewhat assuring a stable flow of income over the specified term in the lease. (I say "somewhat assuring" because you cannot entirely guarantee that a tenant won't move out prematurely, before his or her lease obligations are met.)

A long-term lease has two primary disadvantages: The first is that you've restricted the salability of the property because the lease would take priority over the buyer's occupation rights should you sell the property before the lease expires. (The lease and all rights belonging to it are conveyed if the property is sold.) The second disadvantage is that a long-term lease restricts the amount of rent you can charge (the contractual amount of rent cannot be changed until the term expires).

The alternative is a month-to-month rental agreement. It has the disadvantage of the tenant's being obliged to occupy and pay rent only in monthly increments. However, the advantages are that such a short-term rental does not inhibit the salability of the property, and you're entitled to increase the rent after 30 days.

I recommend using a 12-month lease; not any longer. If you use a term of more than one year, you can seriously inhibit the sale of the leased property. Any term longer than 12 months should have a rent escalation clause drafted into the lease allowing the owner to periodically increase rents to reflect inflation and real estate appreciation.

Simply renting out your property is definitely a proven strategy of realizing a reasonable yield on your investment. However, there's another method that offers greater returns and fewer landlord hassles than simply renting to tenants, and that method is to give the tenants a buy-option.

Renting to Tenants and Giving Them a Buy-Option

If the available unit is *not* part of an apartment complex but instead is a detached single-family dwelling or a condominium, a profitable alternative to renting is to give your tenant an *option to buy*. So, instead of just a standard leasehold agreement, you make a special arrangement giving your tenants an option to buy the house, and you charge them a monthly *option fee* that applies toward the specified purchase price.

For example, say you rent a house for $950 and you give the tenant the option to buy it. In addition to the rent, the tenant pays you $250 a month for the option that applies toward the purchase price. Therefore, instead of collecting just $950 a month in rent, you collect $1,200 a month ($950 plus $250). If the tenant doesn't exercise the option, he or she loses all the applied option fees.

The option to buy is a separate part of the rental agreement, and it specifies the price and terms of the purchase agreement. Under a typical option agreement, the owner (*optionor*) of the property gives the tenant (*optionee*) the right to purchase the rented property at a specified price and terms within a set period of time.

Buy-Option Example

Say, for example, you have a nice three-bedroom, two-bath home you can rent for $950 a month. Why not earn a larger profit by giving the tenant an option to buy the house for $145,000 during the first year of the lease?

Here's how the numbers work (see also Figure 2.1): The tenant pays rent at $950 a month plus $250 a month in option fees, which apply toward the purchase price. If, at the end of a year the tenant wants to exercise the option to buy, he or she has to come up with a down payment of $5,000. He already has applied $3,000 ($250 in option fees × 12 = $3,000), so in addition he needs $2,000 in cash to meet the down payment requirement.

The terms of the purchase can be "installment sale on a land contract" whereby you continue paying on the first mortgage but the tenant-buyer pays you on a land contract at a negotiated rate of interest, preferably higher than the rate of interest you're already paying on the existing mortgage. The tenant-buyer does not get the title to the property

Figure 2.1 Buy-Option Example

Your existing loan payment at 6 percent on a $100,000 mortgage for 30 years equals $1,013 monthly P&I on a house you purchased for $120,000.

After a year of renting, your tenant exercises a buy-option for $145,000 with a $5,000 down payment, and you finance the balance of $140,000 on a land contract at 8 percent for 30 years, or $1,338 monthly P&I. Because of the spread in interest rates ($1,338 versus $1,013), you earn the differential of $325 per month.

The following is a sample of a buy-option contract:

This option to purchase is made and entered into this 1st day of April, 2005, by and between Andy Seller, hereinafter called Landlord (owner), and Fred Buyer, hereinafter called Tenant.

Subject property is a detached single-family residence located at 3750 Arby, Las Vegas, Nevada, 89107.

Landlord hereby agrees to grant an option to purchase to Tenant based on the following terms and conditions: Provided that Tenant shall not then be in default of leased property, Tenant to have the option to purchase subject property at a price of $145,000 for one year beginning April 1, 2005, and expiring March 31, 2006.

Tenant agrees to pay a monthly option fee of $250 during the term of the option, which will be applied toward the purchase price. Tenant further agrees to pay a down payment, including paid option fees, of $5,000 to exercise this option.

Tenant agrees to finance the balance owing of $140,000 on a land contract in favor of the Landlord at 8 percent per annum for 30 years at $1,338 principal and interest per month.

After the option is exercised, Tenant agrees further to pay all taxes, insurance, and mortgage payments into a trust account for disbursement to all parties concerned and pay for such a trust account.

Tenant also (when the option to buy is exercised) agrees to purchase subject property in "as-is" condition.

Landlord agrees to have all loans, taxes, and insurance current at the time of execution of this Option to Buy agreement.

Landlord and Tenant agree to split in half all normal closing costs except that Tenant is to pay for title insurance.

Landlord further agrees to apply all security deposits and cleaning fees under the lease agreement toward the down payment upon execution of this agreement.

The parties hereto have executed this option on this date first above written:

By________________________Landlord

By ___________________________Tenant

until all the terms of the land contract are fulfilled. Furthermore, the tenant-buyer sacrifices all monies already paid if he or she defaults on the terms written in the land contract.

Buy-option strategies can be lucrative tools in real estate investing. They work because they have a broad market appeal to potential tenant-buyers who lack the capacity to purchase a home using traditional methods. Some people who want to buy their own homes don't have the required down payment, or they like the idea of making their down payment on the installment plan (paying monthly option fees that apply toward the down payment.)

Put Everything in Writing

The precise terms of the option must be spelled out in the contract. This way there will be no doubt or further negotiation. The landlord and the tenant-buyer will know exactly who is responsible for what, and for how much.

An option to purchase can be as creative as you want it to be; however, it should be kept relatively simple to avoid any misunderstandings. Should, for instance, your tenant-buyer require a longer term on the option, there are essentially two methods of determining the future selling price for an extended term (longer than one year). After one year, you could set the option price at the one-year price plus 1.5 times the consumer price index (CPI). Then, if the CPI is, say, 4 percent, the selling price after two years would be 1.5 times the 4 percent CPI, or 6 percent higher than the established selling price after one year.

The other alternative is to arbitrarily fix a selling price at which the tenant can buy the property during a specific term, such as $155,000 after two years, and $170,000 after three years.

Structuring and Setup of the Option Agreement

The option agreement should also spell out any arrangements that might be considered unclear, such as the disposition of prepaid deposits (pet and security) and appliances (washer, dryer, and refrigerator). For instance, the cleaning, security, and pet deposits that have been prepaid can be applied toward the down payment. If the landlord has supplied any appliances for the tenant's use with the leased property, the exact disposition of them has to be spelled out in the contract. If they are to be included in the selling price, say so in the option agreement; otherwise, spell out the price you require for such items.

When the time comes for the buy-option tenant to exercise the option, you can open an escrow so that you'll have a neutral third party carrying out the provisions of the agreement according to procedures common for your area. Once the escrow is closed, however, it's important to open a trust account for the protection of both you and the buyer. Most title companies will also operate as a neutral trust.

The purpose of the trust is to act as a neutral third party that will take in the buyer's funds, make all disbursements (loans, taxes, and insurance), then send you a check for what is left over. This assures you and the buyer that everything is taken care of under terms of the contract. You don't have to worry about the taxes or insurance being paid, and the buyer doesn't have to worry about the existing underlying loans being paid.

Land Banking

This strategy is long term in nature because you're investing in a property that you intend to hold and generate rental income on and then at some time in the future convert to a different, more profitable use. For example, in Manhattan you could invest in a parking lot with the intention of building a high-rise office building on the land at some time in the future when demand is high for office space. Meanwhile, you continue to operate the parking lot until the time is appropriate—perhaps when office space is scarce and construction money is available at low or reasonable interest rates—to construct the office building.

Another example of land banking would be building storage rental units on a site that you feel will be very strategic at some future time.

Landlord Tale

When I managed property for a developer in Lansing, Michigan, the owner accomplished the ultimate in land banking. During the 1960s, he converted five locations into thriving McDonald's restaurants, each one set up on a triple-net land lease wherein the tenant pays the taxes, insurance, and cost of maintenance. (One of them was the third McDonald's ever built in the United States.) Each lease specified a minimum rent for the land of $440 per month or 5 percent of the gross monthly sales, whichever was higher. From day 1, McDonald's never did pay the minimum rent: Based on 5 percent of gross sales, each location ended up paying an average of $1,500 per month. That's an average of $18,000 per year in rent income just for the use of the land, on parcels the owner had purchased for less than $10,000 each.

It should be noted that back in the 1960s McDonald's was an up-and-coming enterprise, and at the time it didn't have the financial capacity to purchase land to build their restaurants on. Once they became successful, they could afford to purchase the land required for their restaurants.

Examples could be a key intersection or future site for a freeway exit ramp. Meanwhile, you rent out the storage units with the intention of someday tearing the units down and building something more appropriate (more profitable) on the site, such as a shopping mall. Or you might buy a house on a corner lot in the path of future outward city growth, keeping it rented until, after five years or so, you can convert it to a corner mini-mart or strip mall with lots of tenants paying commercial rents. The reason land banking can be very profitable is because commercial rent is usually twice that of residential rent.

This strategy has a great advantage over investing in similarly located unimproved land because the rented house generates income until growth makes the conversion to a commercial use possible. If you owned land that was just vacant, you would have to pay the mortgage and taxes without the benefit of income. More important, because there would be no improvements on the land, you would have no tax relief because there would be no building to depreciate.

Converting Properties to Other Uses

Converting residential property to commercial usage can be very profitable because commercial space, on average, rents for twice the rate of residential space. Some examples of lucrative conversions can be seen all over a thriving metropolis—near downtown areas you'll see buildings that were once large, older homes converted to office space; what was once a 40-acre farm on the outskirts of town is now a sprawling enclosed shopping mall. And in residential areas you'll see former apartments now serving as condominiums. These are prime examples of conversions in which both land and improvements were adapted to a more profitable usage as the region has grown and changed.

The purpose of making conversions is to upgrade the usage of real estate so that you can earn more profits. Since commercial space usually rents for twice the amount of residential space, it's wise to always be on the lookout for residential properties that can be converted to commercial usage. The following are profitable types of conversions accomplished by innovative investors: Apartments to condominiums, apartments to office space, and house to office space.

Converting Apartments to Condominiums

To make a profit in converting an apartment building into individual condominium units, ideally you need to purchase the apartments cheaply enough so that when you sell each unit eventually as a converted salable condo, the money you receive will be more than you paid for the unit.

The costs of the legal procedures and incidental expenses required to convert an apartment, as well as the value of your own time and effort, are usually figured in a two-to-one ratio: This means that the sales price of the converted condo should be at least twice that of the purchase price for the unit when it was part of the apartment building. For example, if the purchase price of the apartment building is $40,000 per unit, then the sales price of each individual condo will have to be at least $80,000. This two-to-one markup is necessary to absorb the incidental costs incurred, plus the time and effort necessary to make such a conversion.

When figuring the costs of making a particular conversion, you must consider the legal procedures necessary to accomplish a conversion to condominiums. First, the city has to approve the change in property usage. So the city will require you to submit plans explaining exactly how you intend to make the conversion. Should the city consider your plans adequate, it will likely approve them. If not, the city will probably not turn down your request completely but rather make their approval contingent upon your making certain changes that they will specify, such as adding parking or bathrooms. Before you decide to convert apartments to condos, analyze the local area to determine what comparable condos—units that are similar in size, quality, and features that you intend to build—are selling for. If you can purchase an apartment building at a price low enough to make it feasible and profitable for you to renovate and sell the converted units at the two-to-one ratio already mentioned, then by all means go ahead with your plans.

Converting Apartments to Office Space

As mentioned earlier, commercial office space typically rents for twice the rate of comparable residential apartment space. It would therefore appear, at first glance, highly profitable to convert apartments to office space. But before you go ahead with such a conversion, consider some important questions:

- Is the property you wish to convert within a *commercial zone?* If not, can the zoning be easily changed?
- What is the current *vacancy rate* for office space in the area of the subject property? If too much space is already available, it would be unwise to convert.
- Does the property have adequate *parking* for office space? Typically, the city will require one parking space for every 500 square feet of rentable office space.
- How much will it *cost* to convert? Could you borrow the money to finance such a conversion?
- And, finally, will the incidental costs, legal procedures, and time and effort be worth the eventual profit you will realize?

Study the situation carefully. Thoroughly analyze the finances of the projected conversion. Keep in tune with the requirements given, and if you can convert and finance at a reasonable cost and still earn a substantial profit, then go ahead with your plans.

Converting a House to Office Space

Again, based on the premise that commercial rent is usually twice that of residential, converting a house to certain kinds of commercial use can be very profitable. For instance, converting a large house to a law office or a medical clinic offers the investor a lot of opportunity. Of course, not every house is ripe for conversion. The prime candidate should be located on a busy street with enough square footage and land to accommodate a thriving business. In addition, you have to bear in mind that in order to bring about this type of conversion, you will probably need a change in zoning from residential to commercial use.

As an example, on the west side of Las Vegas along Jones Boulevard, there are a number of luxurious ranch homes situated on half-acre lots. In 1986, Jones Boulevard was expanded from a two-lane road to a six-lane boulevard. This change, which added more traffic to this once-quiet neighborhood, caused homeowners there to become disenchanted with their location (no more quiet enjoyment). As a result, many properties along Jones started going up for sale.

An investor then decided to buy one of these lovely ranch homes and convert it to a family dentistry center. This investor made a profit because the situation was perfect for a conversion: homeowners unhappy to find their homes facing a busy boulevard, plus a large good-quality building in a busy location.

As this example shows, you can profit from keeping your eyes open for certain changes occurring in your area. Widening of roads, new interchanges, or other such changes can present opportunity for the shrewd investor who has the ability and the foresight to make profitable conversions.

The Business Plan

You need to write a business plan before you buy. It's important to develop a plan because it forces you to think through the most important factors of owning a particular property. It also compels you to think about your future goals and objectives.

By starting with a business plan before you make any investments, you will have already made some fundamental decisions as to what you're looking for in a particular property. Are you looking for a safe return, or are you looking for a situation in which you're going to buy and do something to the property, perhaps dramatically increasing its value based on your creative vision, and then renting or selling the units to make a profit? Is it going to be a short- or long-term investment?

Your business plan will also serve as a basis for presentations you might need to make to potential lenders and investors.

The Framework for Getting Started

These are the key points to consider in writing a successful business plan:

- What is the purpose of the investment? That is, how does it fit into your long- or short–term overall financial goals and objectives?
- How are you going to increase the value of whatever it is you intend to buy?

- How do you intend to manage the property? Will it be a long-term holding period?
- How will you finance the property? Do you intend to get investors, or will you finance it through a bank by yourself?
- If you need investors, how will you attract them? What will they get?
- How does the financial analysis look for the property? What are the projected fixed costs for refurbishment, the running costs for maintaining it, and the projected income to be generated from it?
- How does the investment timeline look for the property? When does it indicate that expenses will be incurred and income will be received?

You need the business plan to show your lenders or investors the expectations for the project. To do that, it should include all the costs you estimate, including those for acquisition, refurbishment, holding, and financing. And it should give a project time frame, specifying, for example, how long you intend to hold the property. It should also give your potential lenders and investors some background information on how you arrived at your predictions. For example, you could include project charts showing figures for comparable rentals in the vicinity.

Determining the Purpose of the Investment

Land banking is a good example of an extremely long-term investment. What you'll be doing is buying land on the theory that, in time, it's going to go up in value, perhaps because it's in a strategic location. Meanwhile, you're going to pay the taxes on it, and that's your investment. But you don't intend to develop it yourself. You don't intend to build on it. Instead, you intend only to own it, letting it become more valuable as a result of appreciation and inflation by themselves. In New York City, a good example of land banking would be acquiring an existing parking lot. Your intention is to continue running the property as a parking lot, but at some point in the future, you will build a high-rise office building on the site.

You'll find that land banking works very well when there's an area or neighborhood that is in transition or looks like it's in transition. For example, you have a depressed area over here, while an area not far away is starting to flourish, being rebuilt, and rising in value. You could say, "Hey, I can buy here in this depressed area while it's cheap because sooner or later the growth nearby will come my way. And I want to be there when it happens. So I want to buy on the theory that there will be an uptick at some time in the future."

You can't really say how long it will take for that to happen. No one knows for sure. But you can be sure that the earlier you buy it, the cheaper the price will be. And conversely, the later you buy it—once the burgeoning gets real close—the more expensive the price will be because the owner then says, "I can hold it myself, I don't need you!"

How Donald Trump Does It

Here's some savvy advice from one of the world's top real estate developers: How does Donald Trump target a potential real estate investment? According to George Ross, lead author of *Trump Strategies for Real Estate:*

> Donald looks for parcels that are underutilized. He's very much concerned with location. He also carefully estimates how much time and money should be spent on a particular project. And if he lacks certain expertise about something he will brainstorm with someone that has the professional expertise. You have to have someone who has the expertise in what you plan on doing. If you're going to renovate single-family housing, get someone who knows renovation and the costs involved. With the taxes, get a tax expert in order to get the maximum tax benefit of whatever it is your project will be. You always want to look for opportunities to cut costs. Surround yourself with professionalism.
>
> Once Trump makes the evaluation of the target property, and decides whether or not it will work, he then starts to plan how he will go with A, B, C, and D, etc. A: Buy the property, B: get the air rights. C: Must get air rights quietly. D: Make some plans, some models of the proposed building. E: Make some preliminary cost estimates to determine cost feasibility, and what kind of income it would generate.

3

Key Guidelines for Making a Superior Realty Investment

Key Points

- *Eleven key guidelines for making good realty investments*
- *Some time-tested basic advice to keep in mind when buying a home*

Even the newest investor who lacks experience and knowledge in the real estate market can still expect to be able to buy a house or rental property and make a small profit on it given enough time to overcome his or her shortcomings. But to be able to buy a house or rental property and make it a superior investment that yields a great return takes practiced skills and learned strategies. To accomplish this feat, you need proven know-how, and you need to adhere to a specific investment strategy that incorporates the established guidelines to follow. This way you reduce risk and maximize the value of your investment.

Overview of the Key Guidelines

When you know what to look for in a superior realty investment, along with what to avoid, you will have a better chance of being a successful real estate investor. The following is a summary of the 11 key guidelines, after which each is discussed in detail.

1. *Specialize in detached single-family residences*. They are the wisest choice, especially for the newcomer to real estate investing. Avoid investing in condos and co-operative apartments.
2. *Buy bargain-priced undervalued improved property.* In this way you earn a profit because you avoid making a costly mistake—that of paying too much for a property.
3. *Buy property that can be profitably improved.* When investing in property with minor defects that can easily be cured, you add value through cost-effective renovations.
4. *Buy property with low-cost fixed-rate financing.* Don't be lured by lenders' offers of unpredictable and moderate- to high-risk adjustable-rate mortgages or interest-only loans.
5. *Buy from motivated sellers.* Reason: You cannot bargain with an inflexible unmotivated seller.
6. *Buy improved property on a sizable parcel of land.* Avoid speculation in vacant land and small parcels of real estate.
7. *Buy property with a good location in a thriving market.*
8. *Become a great negotiator.* When you can convince the other side to your way of thinking, you will have a big advantage in all your future real estate acquisitions.
9. *Buy when others are afraid to buy.*
10. *Buy during slow periods.*
11. *Buy income properties with below-market rents that can be raised.*

The 11 Key Guidelines

1. Specialize in Detached Single-Family Residences

Specialization is important because one who specializes becomes efficient and is usually very good at what he or she does in a particular profession. Most medical doctors specialize in one particular field of medicine and many attorneys specialize in one particular field of law in order to be an expert in that specialized field. It's much more practical, and probably easier, to be an expert in one specific field of endeavor than to become a jack-of-all-trades, master of none.

And why should you specialize in detached single-family residences (DSFRs)? Because of all the different types of housing—such as attached homes like condominiums and co-operative apartments—DSFRs have historically held their value better in weak markets and have appreciated more in strong booming markets. Moreover, American homeowners have always had a deep-seated love affair with detached homes.

For the small investor, specializing in DSFRs is the wisest choice. There's a plentiful supply along with a strong demand for them created by other small investors and first-time home buyers. The category of attached homes represents less than 10 percent of the overall residential marketplace, and so there is an adequate supply of buyers and demand for homes to make it worth your while. This book does not recommend that you invest in any type of attached home. About the only exception would be a condominium, but only if it can be purchased as a real bargain.

If you stick to learning as much as you can about DSFRs, values in the surrounding neighborhood, and the cost per square foot of detached homes throughout your area, then you have a very great chance of succeeding as a real estate investor.

2. Buy Bargain-Priced Undervalued Improved Property

When you're out prospecting for property to invest in, ask yourself, "Is the property I'm considering purchasing bargain priced? Would other potential buyers like this property? And if I had to, could I sell this property tomorrow and not take a loss?" If you can answer yes to these three questions, then you can be assured that you haven't overpaid for the property and that it has built-in value.

Improved property is land with improvements such as a home or a building built on it. Improved property is a better investment than vacant land because you have the tax relief benefit of depreciating the improvements on the land. The land, by itself, is not depreciable for tax purposes. Another reason vacant land is usually not a good investment is that it's difficult to finance. Commercial lenders consider it speculative, and they tend to shy away from unimproved property.

How to Know If a Property Is Bargain Priced

In order to make superior realty investments, you must evaluate potential acquisitions accurately. You have to recognize a bargain when you see it. Knowing how to precisely determine value, then, is the true nuts-and-bolts skill of profitable realty investing. Conversely, by not using proper appraisal techniques (see Chapter 7, "Appraisals"), you can fall prey to one of the greatest perils in realty investing—that of paying too much for property!

You can easily avoid this pitfall by understanding property values in your local market. Once you become familiar with residential real estate values in your area and are fully informed about recent sales prices, you'll be more efficient at spotting bargain-priced real estate.

Begin by researching the local residential marketplace. Obtain a multiple-listing-service (MLS) book from your Realtor, which covers all property listed for sale in the area. Look up recent sales, and especially take note of the price per square foot of both improved and unimproved residential real estate.

The price per square foot of living space is the most important factor in quickly determining the value of improved real estate. From this information alone, you can usually decide whether a property deserves further attention. For example, if you already know that you can sell a house at $65 per square foot in a particular geographic area, then you can be assured that if you buy a house in that area at $60 per square foot or less, you will have definitely made a wise investment.

Furthermore, you should also become familiar with unimproved land values. Knowing the value of a standard-size vacant residential lot or a half-acre residential lot could prove very useful during your house-hunting treks.

Other ways of becoming familiar with your local marketplace are to check out open houses on weekends and read through the local real estate classified ads.

Keep in mind that before you buy real estate, think about selling—will other potential buyers want to invest in it, and could you resell it tomorrow for what you paid for it today?

3. Buy Property That Can Be Profitably Improved

Does the property have curable defects that can be fixed—without great expense or major effort—to enhance its value enough to earn a reasonable profit? One of the best ways to add value to your investment is to make selective, cost-effective renovations. Some of the easiest defects to correct are cosmetic. Often, the sellers just never bothered to properly clean and maintain the property. Frequently, the only renovations needed are fresh paint, new carpeting, hardwood floor refinishing, and new landscaping. (See Chapter 9 for more details about renovating the fixer-upper.)

Kitchens and Bathrooms Are Key

Every successful builder knows that the most important rooms in houses or apartments, as far as occupants are concerned, are kitchens and bathrooms. Extra dollars spent in these rooms will reap big rewards either in earned rent or selling price. If you're too thrifty with costs in remodeling your kitchen and bathrooms, it will be difficult to attract the upscale tenant or buyer. These two rooms are what sell houses and attract the high-end tenant. Not bedrooms. The first thing a prospective tenant or house buyer looks for are well-designed functional kitchens and bathrooms. There's an old proverb popular among Realtors that goes like this: When a married couple is house hunting and thinking of buying a particular property, the first thing the woman considers is the kitchen and the bathrooms; the man's first consideration is whether or not he can afford the monthly mortgage payment.

4. Buy Property with Low-Cost Fixed-Rate Financing

If you intend to finance the acquisition with a conventional mortgage, you should avoid adjustable-rate mortgages (ARMs) and look for a lender that will offer you a low-cost fixed-rate mortgage. Don't be teased or induced into borrowing long term with an ARM just because the initial interest rate is lower than a fixed-rate mortgage. Over the long haul, fixed-rate mortgages are a safer bet, with less risk for the borrower. (The advantages of fixed-rate mortgages are discussed in detail in Chapter 4.)

Also, will the sellers carry back a low-interest purchase-money mortgage for their equity in the property? Could you arrange to have the sellers accept FHA or VA financing on the property? If so, you could buy the property using any one of the high-leverage owner-occupied investment strategies discussed in Chapter 4.

5. Buy from Motivated Sellers

Why do you want to buy from motivated sellers? Because you cannot bargain with an inflexible seller—someone who, for whatever reason, is not motivated to sell. A motivated seller is more inclined to be flexible with the selling price and terms of the deal. A motivated seller is someone who, because of certain circumstances, is prepared to sell below market value, at favorable terms to the buyer. Such circumstances might include an upcoming divorce, a death in the family, a job relocation, a vacant rental property and/or associated landlord hassles, financial problems, or having already purchased another home that is ready to be moved into. If a seller is in any of these situations or a combination of them, he or she will often be extremely motivated and may be prepared to accept about any reasonable offer.

In contrast, an unmotivated seller can put up serious obstacles to making a good deal. He or she may obstruct the making of a deal because there's nothing pushing him or her to sell. The seller may have a fixed price in mind and come hell or high water, nobody will ever get the property for less.

With so many motivated sellers in the marketplace, there's no reason why you should have to deal with an unyielding seller.

6. Buy Improved Property on a Sizable Parcel of Land

Sizable is key here because you're always better off with more land. Why? Because the more land you have, the more flexibility for expansion or usage you have. More land also makes the property more desirable, which in turn makes it more valuable. In that regard, you have to understand that the improvements on the land—such as the house and garage—of course, have value, but these improvements eventually wear down and become obsolete. It's the land, itself, that over the long haul endures and appreciates in value. Remember too that there's a limited finite supply of habitable land. This means that the growing population (immigration) will continue to put a lot of upward pressure on demand for land, inevitably leading to even higher demand in the future.

Landlord Tale

In 1997 Rose and MJ retired, sold their home, put their furniture in storage, and bought a two-year-old 34-foot motor home. Along with their two miniature French poodles, they traveled full-time throughout the United States visiting friends and family. Eventually Rose tired of all the travel, and they bought a new home along the Mississippi Gulf Coast. They took all their stored furniture and moved it in the house with the intention of selling the motor home. They tried putting it on a recreational vehicle (RV) lot to sell on consignment, but it had no slide outs. Then they discovered another problem: New RVs are financed with no money down, but used RVs require a down payment. And no one wanted a used RV without slide outs. Then when they took it off the consignment lot, they had to pay fees to store it.

The problem was that they didn't have enough land to park the motor home on. They ended up having to pay $75 a month to store it when they could have kept it on their property had they had more land.

Lack of sufficient land inhibits the growth potential of the property. Back in the early 1980s when I first started to buy real estate in Las Vegas, Nevada, I discovered that the best bargains were to be found investing in homes on large parcels of land. In particular, I began specializing in middle-class homes built on lots that were at least a half-acre in size. The reason was that I could get more for my money, particularly more land. I found that the sellers of these half-acre properties usually overlooked the precise value of the land. In other words, frequently I could buy a 1,600- to 2,000-square-foot home on a half-acre for about the same price as a similar tract home on one-fourth the amount of land.

7. Buy Property with a Good Location in a Thriving Market

Another key guideline to making a superior investment is looking for property in a good location in a thriving market. Much has been said over the years about the importance of location as the prime consideration when investing in real estate. This is most certainly true when investing in a home for yourself, but it is not always the case when purchasing investment property.

An investment property should be a better-than-average moneymaker that appreciates in value. The subject property you're interested in may not be in the best part of town, but if it's a moneymaker, don't let the location stop you from making a sound investment. In other words, just because you wouldn't live there yourself, don't let the location detract from what otherwise would be a good investment.

A "Good Location" Means in a District with Good Schools

Whether you have school-age children or not, you always want to buy in a district with good-quality schools. Reason: When it comes time to rent or sell, you'll learn that strong school districts are a top priority among both renters and home buyers, which helps to increase rents and property values.

Location No-Nos

Instead of knowing what to look *for* in a location, sometimes it's better to be aware of what to *avoid* in a location. Be careful of buying residential property in a neighborhood that has certain nuisances that may detract from the value. Before purchasing residential property, ask the following questions:

- Is it located in a floodplain and subject to floods?
- Is it located next to a commercial building, such as a warehouse or factory?
- Is it adjacent to a cemetery or an undertaker?
- Is it near an airport or under the flight path of incoming or departing aircraft?
- Does an unusual volume of vehicular traffic pass nearby that may prove to be a nuisance?
- Is it next to a school playground, where noisy children may interfere with the quiet enjoyment of the premises?

These characteristics of a location detract from the value of residential property. You can avoid these nuisances by carefully checking out the surrounding neighborhood before committing yourself to a long-term investment such as real estate.

Besides the location, you also have to be concerned with whether or not your subject property is within a thriving market. Generally speaking, a *thriving market* is one that's not declining in population, employment, and property values.

One example of a nonthriving market, or declining area, was the city of Houston, Texas, in the late 1980s. During that time Houston experienced what economists call a "rolling recession." A glut of petroleum supplies on the world market caused oil prices to fall drastically. This resulted in oil companies cutting back on employment, with many related businesses failing as well. Also, many banks failed during this time, partially because of home mortgages that many unemployed people living in Houston could no longer make payments on. The result was an oversupply of housing and foreclosures, as many of the unemployed moved away to find work elsewhere. Eventually, the overall value of real estate in the Houston area dropped dramatically because of this rolling recession.

You should also be wary of investing in smaller urban areas that depend primarily on one type of industry. This is because if that particular employer experiences bad economic times or has to shut down operations, the surrounding area will inevitably become depressed. On the other hand, areas that have diverse industries, such as Los Angeles or Boston, do not depend economically on one particular industry for employment. These urban areas will thrive even if one major industry fails.

Always Consider the Logistics

The home should be within a reasonable commute to and from the workplace. Consider too that residential property should always be in a good proximity to shopping, restaurants, and entertainment. Potential tenants or buyers will be turned off by property that is poorly situated in relation to these amenities.

8. Become a Great Negotiator

The art of negotiation is more than just haggling over price and terms. It involves preplanning, knowing human nature, and uncovering weaknesses and learning how to exploit them. Moreover, it's the ability to counter your adversary's tactics, such as knowing when to ignore the so-called bogus buyer, and not being misled by the "look of legitimacy."

If you can adopt some of negotiation principles and tactics offered in this book, you will give yourself a big advantage in your future real estate acquisitions. See Chapter 8 for more details about the principles of negotiation and high-powered tactics.

9. Buy When Others Are Afraid to Buy

Residential real estate historically goes through cycles of boom and bust. The trend is usually predominantly upward, but once in a while the demand for housing can decline. This slowdown, or "bust," in the housing market usually occurs after a runup in interest rates, which is also associated with an economy in recession, along with high unemployment, fewer home buyers in the marketplace, and a large supply of homes for sale. This so-called buyer's market inevitably results in declining real estate prices. Yet, for the shrewd investor who has faith in the marketplace and knows that, in time, the economy has to get better—that interest rates will fall, that unemployment will decrease, and that more home buyers will return to the marketplace—the situation presents a great opportunity. Because if everybody else is afraid to buy, then you don't have as much competition, and you can choose from a larger inventory of homes for sale at reduced prices.

10. Buy During Slow Periods

With little exception, during a typical 12-month year, real estate markets experience predictable busy and slow periods. Just as it's shrewd to buy when real estate prices are depressed, likewise it can be worthwhile to buy during these typical slow and inactive periods.

For example, the period from mid-November through February of the next year is typically very slow in most real estate markets. There is less activity in the dead of winter, as many snowbirds are vacationing in the warm southern states while others are busy celebrating the holidays with family. Moreover, in certain areas such as the colder, northernmost regions of the country, these inactive periods can extend into April. However, in other regions where it's warmer year-round, like Florida and the desert southwest, home-buying activity revs up as early as February.

It's to your advantage to buy during these inactive periods since there are fewer buyers to compete with. And those who have their properties for sale during these slow periods tend to be motivated sellers.

This does not mean, however, that you should look for bargains only during these inactive periods. The majority of real estate for sale is put on the market during the most active period of March through early November, which means a wider selection of inventory is available then, and of course, there will be fewer properties to choose from during the inactive period.

11. Buy Income Property with Below-Market Rents That Can Be Raised

If you can find an underrented apartment building, assuming everything else is in order, you have found a great potential property to invest in. Why? Because you won't have to spend a fortune to improve the property. Instead, essentially all you have to do to increase its value is raise the rents up to the level where they should be.

Here's an example: Let's say you found a property for sale with eight two-bedroom units renting $200 per month below market (that is, below what they should be renting for). Eight units at a $200 per month increase is $1,600. Multiply the monthly rent by 12 to get an annual rental increase of $19,200. If we deduct a 5 percent vacancy loss, the result is an increase in net operating income (NOI) of $18,240. If we capitalize the amount of increased income by 10 percent, the result is an increase in value of $182,400 simply by increasing the rent of each unit by $200.

If the property you purchase is within these proposed guidelines, the probability is high that it will be a very profitable realty investment. And consider too the following special basic advice for successful home buying.

Some Time-Tested Basic Advice to Keep in Mind When Buying a Home

The following advice is mostly general and fundamental, to offer you a better overall perspective of the home-buying process. Some of them are common mistakes novice home buyers often make:

- *The best time to consider the sale of your house is before you buy it.* When looking at prospective purchases, take into consideration the features and amenities of the home that other buyers would find desirable. In other words, pretend you are looking at the home's amenities through the eyes of other buyers. If you don't, it will be difficult to find a buyer or get a good price when you sell it.
- *Be aware that for most people buying a home is a very emotional experience.* The better prepared you are—knowing comparable values (cost per square foot of similar properties) and prevailing mortgage interest rates along with how much house you can afford—the easier it will be to control your emotions and make a better deal.
- *Remember that everything is negotiable.* Shrewd buyers are fully informed of market conditions and neighborhood values. They also know when it's wise to make a lowball offer, and they realize that there are situations when it's best to make the initial offer the best offer they can afford.
- *Never ignore logistics.* Carefully consider the commute to and from the workplace. A home should be enjoyed, not despised because travel to and from the workplace is spent as wasted time in gridlocked traffic. Consider too the home's proximity in relation to grocery shopping, restaurants, and entertainment.
- *Never buy if you can't stay put.* If you cannot commit to remaining in one place for five years or more, then owning a home is probably not for you. The short-term costs of buying and selling are prohibitive over a very short term. And renting it out and maintaining the property as an absentee landlord is not recommended because it is too difficult to oversee from far away, and you lose direct control when you must hire a property management company to oversee it in your absence.
- *Never be an absentee landlord.* You never want to hand over the management responsibility of your property unless you can directly oversee the manager. And you cannot directly oversee a resident manager or a management company if you're an absentee landlord—someone who lives out of state or who resides far enough

away from the property that they cannot visit the property at least once a month. The reason is that there are too many ways unscrupulous people can take advantage of you. For instance, they could claim a unit is vacant when in fact it's occupied while the manager pockets the rent. Or they can charge the absentee landlord for "invisible" repairs that are never done while the owner pays for them and the manager pockets the money. And if you're not there to oversee all this criminal activity, how can you prove it occurred?

Now that you have a grasp of the key guidelines that make a superior realty investment, and you know how to avoid common home-buying mistakes, let's look at various alternatives available for financing your prospective realty investments.

4

Financing Real Estate

The Best Alternatives to Borrowing the Money You Need

Key Points

- *Why it's important to use the most productive type of financing for your real estate investments*
- *A brief history of mortgage lending*
- *The best choice: A fixed-rate amortized loan*
- *Adjustable-rate mortgages (ARMs)*
- *The principle of leverage*
- *Guidelines for borrowing money*
- *Alternatives to the mortgage loan*
- *30-year or 15-year term?*
- *Special types of financing*
- *Maximize leverage with special loan programs for owner-occupants*
- *Loan sources for those with poor credit*

- *Shopping for a mortgage loan*
- *The loan application process*
- *Get preapproved before house hunting*
- *Loan-underwriting standards*

The Financing Is Crucial

Borrowing money from commercial lenders to invest in real estate is one of the most crucial elements in any real estate transaction. The use of borrowed money to buy real estate serves several purposes: It gives you more leverage, which enables you to purchase much more, often 20 or 30 times, than what you could buy otherwise for cash; it reduces your equity exposure; and your interest payments on the loan serve as a great tax deduction.

But there's more to successfully financing real estate than just shopping for a better interest rate. You also should know how to establish relationships with lenders, how to determine how much to borrow, and how to decide between using a fixed- or adjustable-rate loan. These are all instrumental to successfully investing in real estate, regardless of the project's scale.

Most of the Cost Is in the Financing

The most expensive thing that you'll likely ever buy is not your home—it's the cost of the *financing* required to purchase that home. If you take out a mortgage loan to buy your home, as most of us do, the cost of the financing, by itself is the costliest item in the purchase.

Many home buyers are often so concerned with the monthly payment or the price of the home that they fail to take into consideration the aggregate interest cost over the term of the mortgage. They should, and here's why.

Suppose, for instance, that you buy a $120,000 home with a $10,000 down payment, and you finance the balance owing $110,000, with a 7 percent fixed-rate mortgage for 30 years. The monthly principal and interest payment is only $732, but the aggregate amount you will pay over the 30-year term is 360 payments (12 months × 30 years), which multiplies to $263,520. If you deduct the principal paid of $110,000, the result is $153,520 in interest paid. So over a period of 30 years you actually will have paid $263,520 for a $120,000 house. That's a substantial amount of money, and it is more than twice the original price of the home.

But if you learn how to take full advantage of today's financing methods, you can save tens of thousands of dollars on a long-term mortgage. By following the guidelines set forth in this chapter, you can avoid the costliest mistake many home buyers make—paying too much for the wrong financing.

A 1 Percent Differential Can Save You Tens of Thousands

From Figure 4.1, look at how much you can save in interest charges going from 8 to 7 percent on a $110,000 loan over 30 years. As you can see in the figure, over a 30-year term, during which the borrower makes 360 monthly payments, the differential is $75.31 per month, which equals a total savings of $27,112.

Save on Loan Fees Too

Besides shopping for a better rate of interest, there are savings to be earned in the amount of fees that primary lenders charge to originate a mortgage loan. The loan origination fee—usually one-quarter of 1 percent to 2 percent of the loan amount—is the most significant fee the borrower has to pay. You need to shop around to find out how much various lenders in your area charge. On a $160,000 loan, a savings of just 1 point in the origination fee can save you $1,600 when the loan is funded.

And you can save on the cost of private mortgage insurance (PMI) if your down payment on the purchased property is at least 20 percent.

Figure 4.1 Effect of a 1-Point Change in Margin on a $110,000 Loan

	Lender	
Factor	A	B
One-year Treasury index	5%	5%
Margin	+2	+3
Interest rate the borrower pays	7%	8%
Monthly payment	$731.83	$807.14
Difference in payment between A and B = $75.31		

Anything less will cost you an additional $40 to $100 per month in PMI, depending on the amount of the loan.

A Brief History of Mortgage Lending

Besides shopping for the best interest rate, you also need to choose the best type of loan for your particular needs. In today's mortgage marketplace you have a full range of loan alternatives, but essentially you just have two types of interest rates to choose from—adjustable rates and fixed rates. But it wasn't long ago when borrowing money to buy real estate was done very differently.

Before the Great Depression, the interest-only loan was the most common method of financing real estate. Many borrowers took out these loans for short terms, expecting to renew them term after term, thus deferring payment of the principal almost indefinitely. But the world economy severely faltered during the Great Depression that began in 1929, and most lenders were unable to roll over, or perpetuate, these interest-only loans. The results were devastating. Lenders began "calling" loans—that is, requiring borrowers to pay back the entire principal amount—which the borrowers could not pay. Lenders then started foreclosing on these loans throughout the country, which unfortunately was comparable to pouring gasoline on a burning fire, and that only helped to deepen the depression.

As a result of seeing so many foreclosures, almost everyone, especially those within the financial industry, became aware of the inherent dangers of making interest-only loans. A more practical form of loan soon materialized—the fully amortized fixed-rate loan. Once the fully amortized fixed-rate loan became popular, the borrower only had two choices: a 30-year or a 15-year term.

Nowadays, however, mortgage lenders offer a wide range of different types of loans to finance real estate, and notably, some of these loans can be very risky for the borrower. Among them are *graduated loans*—the payment starts low and graduates higher over its term—and *adjustable-rate loans*—the payment and rate of interest are initially low (called a *teaser rate*) and are tied to a certain rate established by the Federal Reserve Board (the Fed) and allowed to fluctuate over the loan term. Then there's the safest type of loan for the borrower, the traditional *fixed-rate loan* that remains "fixed" at a specified rate of interest over the loan's term.

The Best Choice: A Fixed-Rate Amortized Loan

A great alternative to the interest-only loan and the unpredictable graduated loan or an adjustable-rate mortgage is the amortized loan that comes with a fixed rate of interest, featuring equal monthly payments of both principal and interest over the loan's term. So, with the fixed-rate mortgage (as the name suggests), you have a rate that is unchanged during the entire term of the loan. This means you don't have to deal with feelings of anxiety or uncertainty about future changes in your interest rate, which would inevitably lead to changes in your monthly payments.

The problem with all the non-fixed-type loans, such as the graduated and adjustable-rate loans, is that they're too unpredictable. You don't know the rate of interest you'll be paying over the term of the loan. In other words, the initial rate is lower, which is the so-called *teaser rate* that entices you, but as time passes, your adjustable rate can go up or down (though it always seems to go up). The banks love them because if market rates go up, they can raise the rates they charge borrowers, which takes much of the risk out of lending money over the long term. And notably, some naïve borrowers may be enticed by the adjustable-rate loan because the initial interest rate is lower than it would be for a comparable fixed-rate loan, and the home buyer can qualify to borrow more (because of the lower initial rate).

Fixed-rate mortgages favor the borrower because they're predictable—you know what to expect over the entire term of the loan. Conversely, adjustable-rate mortgages favor the lender and are detrimental to the borrower because the interest rates change with market credit conditions.

Take, for example, an adjustable-rate mortgage that starts out at 5 percent. Five years after the initial funding of the loan, the credit market tightens, and that causes interest rates to be raised. So the lender raises the interest rate on the loan to 9 percent. Look what happens during that five-year period: On a $120,000 loan amortized over 30 years, the monthly payment at 5 percent starts at $644. At 9 percent the monthly payment rises to $966, an increase of $322 per month. Many people are simply not prepared to handle the added financial burden of a situation like this.

Example of an amortized-loan payoff: Here's an example of an amortized loan of $90,000 at 6 percent interest with a term of 30 years. The first payment (of a total of 360 over 30 years) for principal and interest is $540, of which $450 goes toward interest and $90 goes toward principal. Payment number 2 is also $540, but because the principal balance owed has been reduced by $90 and is now $89,910, the monthly interest is only $449.55, and so $90.45 is applied toward the principal. And every month thereafter the monthly interest amount is reduced because the amount of borrowed principal is also reduced.

Adjustable-Rate Mortgages (ARMs)

Primary mortgage lenders prefer borrowers to choose an ARM over a fixed-rate loan. Why? Because a fixed-rate mortgage is risky for the lender because it cannot *adjust* to market conditions over the long term. The key word here is "adjust," because it is the reason ARMs were created—for the purpose of protecting long-term lenders from radical changes in market interest rates.

Traditionally, long-term mortgage lenders loaned their money at reasonable interest rates, and rightly so, as their cost of acquiring that money seldom fluctuated. But along came the hyperinflation of the mid-1970s and the early 1980s, when the cost of money went up drastically. When this occurred, the primary lenders had billions of dollars that they had loaned out at interest rates substantially below what it cost them to acquire the funds. To prevent such losses in the future, primary lenders created the ARM.

Noteworthy

In September 1981, the market rate for fixed-rate 30-year mortgages reached an all-time high of 17 percent.

How ARMs Work

ARMs vary somewhat, but they're essentially similar in how they are set up. The initial rate (the so-called teaser rate) is allowed to fluctuate (along with your monthly payment) every one, three, or five years, over the term of the loan. The period from one rate change to the next is referred to as the *adjustment period.* Thus, an adjustable-rate loan with an adjustment period of one year is called a *one-year ARM*.

Most ARMs are based on a formula that includes an *index* and a *margin* (amount of profit). When the index rate moves up or down, so does your adjustable interest rate, along with your monthly payment. There are limits, however, on how much your interest rate can change at any one time, and over the life of the adjustable loan. The interest rate change is usually limited to a maximum of 2 percent during each adjustment period, and an overall cap is placed on the interest increase.

Primary lenders use indexes tied to some easily monitored rate, such as the U.S. Treasuries security rate. Then the lender applies a margin to the index used. The interest rate a lender quotes you on an ARM is equal to the index rate plus the lender's margin.

Given all this, one might wonder why anyone would consider taking out an adjustable-rate loan for an extended term of 15 or 30 years. The answer is that many first-time home buyers and home buyers who are trading up tend to stretch their budgets and force themselves into accepting ARMs. They're actually lured by the ARM's initial lower interest rate because it appears cheaper, and such a mortgage enables the borrower to qualify for a higher loan amount. But look what happens if interest rates increase over the years, which they're likely to do. Ultimately, the borrower will be faced with increased loan payments, which they may or may not be able to pay.

About the only time I would recommend taking out an ARM to finance real estate is when you intend to borrow for a short term: three years or less. Compared to a fixed-rate mortgage, a short-term ARM could be practical and cost effective because of the initial below-market interest rate, which would save you money. The savings on lower interest charges for most ARMs come in the first one to three years, and these loans are usually lower in total cost than a comparable fixed-rate loan.

On the other hand, if you expect to stay in your home and pay on the mortgage more than three years, a fixed-rate loan would be more sensible, especially when you're not in the position to endure the uncertainty associated with an ARM.

Convertible ARMs

Another alternative for short-term borrowers is a hybrid adjustable-rate mortgage that starts out at a fixed rate of interest and then converts to an adjustable-rate loan after a certain period. Typically, the convertible ARM stays at a fixed rate of interest for a period of five years, then adjusts every year thereafter.

The Principle of Leverage

It makes good business sense to borrow as much as you can for as long as you can when investing in real estate. To use leverage in real estate means to invest a small amount of cash (a down payment) to acquire a significantly greater value in property, instead of investing all cash. For instance, a purchase that is 90 percent leveraged would combine a 10 percent down payment with 90 percent financing. Zero leverage would be a full-cash purchase with no financing involved. Due to the impact of inflation and the ever-growing demand for a finite supply of real estate, which, among other factors, causes appreciation, you can achieve the greatest yield on your invested dollars by getting as much leverage as possible when investing in improved real estate.

To see how leverage is used, let's look at a realty investment using 90 percent leverage (a 10 percent down payment) as opposed to purchasing the same property with zero leverage. Suppose you purchase a property for $100,000 with a $10,000 down payment (10 percent), and a year later you realize an increase in value of 10 percent. Therefore, the property is now worth $110,000. Because you put only $10,000 down on the property and it appreciated $10,000, you realized a 100 percent return on investment ($10,000 return divided by $10,000 invested).

Now suppose you could purchase the same property with $100,000 cash (zero leverage), and a year later that property also increased in value to $110,000. In this scenario your investment is $100,000, the appreciation is still \$10,000, but the return (yield) on the investment is only 10 percent (\$10,000 return divided by \$100,000 investment). From the example given it's easy to see that the use of leverage to invest in real estate produces a much higher yield.

Leverage expands yield exponentially. Here's even better news. In the previous examples of the use of leverage, we used only an appreciation factor, which we divided by cash investment to arrive at yield (return on investment). Look at an even more important way leverage can expand your returns and help you pyramid your wealth faster.

Besides appreciation, your rental properties also generate income, which can be factored in to arrive at a total return on investment (ROI). See the following two examples using a 10 percent down payment compared to an all-cash purchase, with a constant net operating income (NOI) and using 4 and 8 percent rates of appreciation:

$$\text{ROI} = \frac{\text{appreciation} + \text{income}}{\text{cash invested}}$$

Example 1: \$100,000 all-cash purchase with \$10,000 NOI and (a) 4 percent and (b) 8 percent rate of appreciation:

$$\text{(a)} \quad \frac{\$4{,}000 + \$10{,}000}{\$100{,}000} = 14\%\ \text{ROI}$$

$$\text{(b)} \quad \frac{\$8{,}000 + \$10{,}000}{\$100{,}000} = 18\%\ \text{ROI}$$

Example 2: \$100,000 purchase price using a \$10,000 down payment with \$10,000 NOI and (a) 4 percent and (b) 8 percent rate of appreciation:

$$\text{(a)} \quad \frac{\$4{,}000 + \$10{,}000}{\$10{,}000} = 140\%\ \text{ROI}$$

$$\text{(b)} \quad \frac{\$8{,}000 + \$10{,}000}{\$10{,}000} = 180\%\ \text{ROI}$$

Keep in mind that even giant blue-chip corporations, such as General Electric and IBM, who have a surplus of cash on hand and who could easily pay cash, instead use leverage to finance their real estate purchases to increase their return on investment.

This principle of leverage in realty investing brings up another important point: Large amounts of income-producing mortgage debt—not consumer debt—can actually be a good wealth-building tool.

Guidelines for Borrowing Money

The wise use of credit is crucial to successful realty investing. Think of it as forming a sort of hypothetical partnership with your lender, but unlike a true partnership, you don't have to pay your partner a share of the profits—just interest on the money you borrowed from them.

Incur Mortgage Debt, but Avoid Consumer Debt

In real estate, mortgage debt is good because it's usually associated with high leverage and sometimes with generating income (rent), which pays off the mortgage debt. On the other hand, consumer debt—credit cards, etc.—is a liability that usually does not generate income, and it therefore becomes a serious burden to the debtor.

A person who has high mortgage debt is usually a debtor who owns plenty of income-producing real estate that pays down the mortgage loans. For example, let's say you buy a four-unit apartment building for $160,000 with a $16,000 down payment, and you take out a mortgage for the balance owing of $144,000. The debt service, property taxes, and insurance add up to $1,350 a month, but each of the units rents for $500 a month. Therefore, your monthly gross income is $2,000. Deduct your basic fixed expenses and debt service ($1,350), and you have a gross operating income of $650 per month. So the income you are collecting pays off the mortgage loan. In other words, you're paying off the debt with other people's money.

Again, in order to succeed and profit at realty investing, you must view the financing of real estate as a joint venture with your lenders. As an investor, however, you don't have to share with the lender the profits you realize; you're only required to pay them interest for the use of their money. In other words, the debt you incur on a particular property is not really a debt you'll pay back with *your* hard-earned money but actually a debt that will generate income and appreciation with which you'll pay back the lender and earn a subsequent profit for yourself.

Borrow As Much As You Can for As Long As You Can

The logic behind this principle is pretty much straightforward. If, after you have taken out a mortgage loan, the credit market eases (interest rates decline) and you have the right of prepayment without penalty, you can effectively refinance at a lower interest rate and save money. If the credit market tightens (interest rates rise), you don't have to worry about refinancing because the rate of interest you're paying is likely lower than the higher prevailing market rate of interest.

This principle also has a lot to do with timing your purchase. Many indecisive people may be inclined to wait for interest rates to come down, thinking if they wait long enough, they can get a better deal on a loan. Meanwhile, the property they were interested in buying is snapped up by someone else, and an opportunity is lost. You must realize that it's very difficult to predict which direction interest rates are headed. You're better off borrowing as much as you can for as long as you can, and then letting the market take care of itself. Remember, if the credit market eases, you can always refinance; and if it tightens, then you can feel good about already having a rate that's below the prevailing interest rate.

How Much Can You Borrow?

For a quick gauge, many primary lenders traditionally use the *gross income multiplier*. A conservative lender might use a multiplier of 2.5 times the borrower's annual gross income, while a more liberal lender might go as high as 3 times. So if you earn a gross annual income of $40,000, using the 2.5 multiplier you could afford to borrow $100,000, and using the 3 multiplier, you could borrow $120,000. Of course, these quick formulas don't take into consideration the borrower's other monthly debt obligations. And mortgage lenders want to be careful that your home loan, including the monthly cost of homeowner's insurance and property taxes, is not greater than you can reasonably afford.

To arrive at a more precise *affordable* home loan, this book reflects the guidelines of most primary lenders. They permit a total debt-to-income ratio of no more than 36 percent. Total debt payments include all monthly payments toward any kind of consumer debt, such as car loans and credit cards, plus the mortgage payment that covers the added cost

Figure 4.2 Mortgage Qualification Guidelines

Annual Gross Income	Monthly Gross Income	29 Percent of Gross Income
$15,000	$1,250	$ 363
20,000	1,667	483
25,000	2,083	604
30,000	2,500	725
35,000	2,917	846
40,000	3,333	967
45,000	3,750	1,088
50,000	4,167	1,208

Source: U.S. Department of Housing and Urban Development.

of homeowner's insurance and property taxes. The guidelines assume a housing payment-to-income ratio of 28 percent for a conservative estimate (the limit you'd expect from a conventional lender), and 29 percent for the aggressive one (the limit allowed on FHA-insured loans). Figure 4.2 lists the 29 percent ratio for different annual and monthly income levels.

When you calculate how much you can borrow, keep in mind that primary lenders look at only your current financial condition when they qualify you. They're unaware of any future financial plans you may have, such as paying for your child's college education or financing a new car. You need to make allowances for these big anticipated expenditures and decide how much of your future income you can realistically commit to housing, so you don't put a strain on your budget.

Avoid Balloon Payments and Prepayment Penalties

A *balloon payment* is a lump sum due at the end of a loan obligation. Essentially it's a promise to pay an additional amount of cash at some future time. If the promise isn't kept, it most certainly will cause a foreclosure. Most commonly you might find a balloon payment due at the end of a loan term that is not fully amortized.

In other words, let's say you buy a property and arrange with the seller to pay on a purchase-money mortgage for the balance owing, which is $20,000. Terms of the mortgage are as follows: Mortgage loan of

$20,000 amortized over 30 years, with the balance payable in full after 10 years, payable with interest at 7 percent in monthly payments of $132. The balloon payment in this case would be the amount of principal owed after 10 years.

If you must obligate yourself to a balloon payment, extend the term as far in the future as possible. This makes the balloon payment easier to live with because you'll have more time to prepare for the payoff.

Prepayment Penalties

This type of penalty clause is written into a loan agreement to entitle the lender to charge the borrower a penalty for premature payoff of the loan. The penalty is usually in the range of 6 to 12 months' interest on the loan. Make sure the mortgage loan you arrange does not have such a clause written into your document—otherwise, you could be penalized thousands of dollars if, for whatever reason, if you decide to prepay or refinance the loan before its term ends.

Both the balloon payment and the prepayment penalty are items that benefit only the lender, not the borrower. These items too can inhibit the sale of your property because under a loan assumption, the buyer would be responsible for the lump-sum payoff on the balloon payment and the prepayment penalty.

Alternatives to the Mortgage Loan

Real estate loans are divided into two categories: loans insured or guaranteed by the federal government (and in some cases the state government) and loans that are not. The most common government-backed loans are sponsored by the Veterans Administration (VA) or the Federal Housing Administration (FHA). Home loans made without government sponsorship are termed *conventional loans.*

Conventional Loans

Compared to the guaranteed VA loan and the insured FHA loan, the conventional loan usually has more stringent qualification standards. The following are special features of a typical conventional loan:

- The minimum down payment required is between 5 and 20 percent.

- If the down payment is less than 20 percent, lender requires the borrower to pay private mortgage insurance (PMI), which costs about half a point.
- The loan is usually not assumable.
- There is not as much red tape, and it can usually be funded faster than nonconventional loans.

Private Mortgage Insurance (PMI)

With conventional loans, borrowers with less than a 20 percent down payment are required to buy insurance that protects the lender against default. PMI costs about half a point of the loan amount (about $40 to $100 per month), and it is added to the borrower's required monthly payment.

The reason conventional lenders require PMI is because the operatives in the secondary mortgage market require it. And in order for mortgage lenders to sell their loans in the secondary mortgage market, they must meet certain standards. One of those standards is for the home borrower to have a minimum down payment of 20 percent; if the down payment is less, PMI is required to insure the differential.

Tip

After you've paid on the mortgage for a few years and your equity in the home is at least 20 percent, you're entitled to cancel the PMI policy and pocket the savings. Note that you must initiate the cancellation. (Many homeowners are not aware of this entitlement and needlessly continue to pay this premium over the full term of the loan.)

The Secondary Mortgage Market

Besides the primary mortgage market, which is the interaction of the realty borrower with the lender who originates the mortgage loan, there also exists a secondary mortgage market that gives liquidity and flexibility to the overall mortgage lending system. When someone buys a loan that he or she did not originate, he or she is engaging in secondary mortgage market activity.

Operatives in the secondary mortgage market will buy lenders' mortgages, thus supplying them with needed cash to originate new loans. Before its creation, primary lenders were often faced with problems of liquidity. For example, suppose a primary lender originates a 30-year mortgage. Although the lender will ultimately recover the principal and earn a substantial amount of interest on the transaction, for 30 years the lender will have tied up a substantial portion of their assets. These assets, which otherwise might have been available for other, possibly more lucrative loans, are in effect frozen. And if the same primary lender invests all their assets in mortgages having similar durations, they most definitely will find themselves in an illiquid position. Thus, the dilemma of liquidity is overcome by the buying and selling of mortgage loans in the secondary mortgage market.

The following are the principal operatives in the secondary mortgage market:

Federal National Mortgage Association (FNMA), referred to as "Fannie Mae," was formed in 1938 for the purpose of buying and selling government-insured mortgages.

Government National Mortgage Association (GNMA), referred to as "Ginnie Mae," was founded in 1968, and it is administered by the U.S. Department of Housing and Urban Development.

Federal Home Loan Mortgage Corporation (FHLMC), referred to as "Freddie Mac," was founded in 1971, and it functions for the purpose of buying and selling of mortgages originated by savings and loans.

Mortgage Guaranty Insurance Corporation (MGIC) is a private entity referred to as "Maggie Mae."

FHA-Insured Loans

The Federal Housing Administration (FHA) assists home buyers who might not be able to meet the higher down payment requirements and qualifying standards used for conventional loans. The FHA works through local lending institutions to provide federal mortgage insurance for the purchase, rehabilitation, or improvement of affordable housing.

Anyone with a reasonable credit history is eligible for an FHA loan. The minimum down payment requirement is 3 percent, and the borrower is permitted to finance the closing costs and the required mortgage insurance premium, which are added to the monthly payment. Eligible properties are one- to four-unit residential structures.

The following are features of the FHA-insured loans:

- You can borrow with as little as 3 percent down.
- The credit qualification standards are not as stringent as they are for conventional financing.
- There is no prepayment penalty.
- The loan is assumable, with qualifications.

VA-Guaranteed Loans

A Veterans Administration (VA) loan is made by a primary lender, such as a bank or savings and loan. Instead of insuring the loan as the FHA does, the VA guarantees the loan against default. The VA's guarantee is intended to encourage primary lenders to offer veterans loans with favorable terms.

Qualified veterans can use a VA loan to buy, build, improve, or refinance an existing home. Ease of qualification and no down payment requirement are the hallmarks of this great benefit, offered to those men and women who have served honorably in the U.S. military. All you need is your form DD-214 (Proof of Discharge). Send it to the VA, and you get back a Certificate of Eligibility. Take your certificate to a lender that makes VA loans and get preapproved. The local VA office can provide more details.

The following are the features of the VA loan:

- As of this writing, you could borrow up to $203,000 with no money down.
- There's no prepayment penalty.
- No PMI is required.
- There's a limit on closing costs charged to the borrower.
- The loan is assumable, with qualifications.

The No-Verification Loan

Nowadays, if you have a good credit history, you can qualify for a "no-verification" loan. They're designed for people who have difficulty in verifying income or assets.

Before the emergence of this type of loan, mortgage lenders required all kinds of documentation from the loan applicant. This included proof of income, tax returns, W2s, bank statements, and job verification. In contrast, under the streamlined program for no-verification loans, the applicant simply states the amount of income he or she earns. However, the lender will usually require one form of verification: a letter from an accountant stating that he or she prepared the borrower's federal income taxes for the last two years.

The mortgage rate is determined by the loan-to-value position in the property and the credit score of the borrower. Also, there are different levels of no-verification loans. There are *stated income, no income*, and *no job* (essentially no named source of income). The difference among these levels is the type of income verification the customer provides. Usually, the less verification, the greater the rate and/or down payment required.

30-Year or 15-Year Term?

Besides choosing which type of financing that's best suited to your needs, you have to decide which term you favor: 30 years or 15 years? Figure 4.3 compares the two.

On a $110,000 loan at 9 percent, the monthly mortgage payments are as follows:

15-year term = $1,115.69   30-year term = $804.62

The differential in monthly payment between the 15- and 30-year loans is $311.07.

As Figure 4.3 indicates, the 15-year term is ideal for those who can afford the higher monthly payments. And compared to the 30-year term,

Figure 4.3 Comparison of Accrued Equity and Interest Paid on 15- and 30-Year Fixed-Rate Mortgages

Loan Amount = $110,000 at 9% Fixed Rate

	15-Year Accrued		30-Year Accrued	
Time	Interest Paid	Equity Earned	Interest Paid	Equity Earned
After 5 years	$45,051	$ 21,890	$ 43,767	$ 4,510
After 15 years	90,824	110,000	122,061	22,770
After 30 years	—	—	179,663	110,000

it saves over $89,000 in interest payments, and notably, lenders usually charge a half-point lower rate of interest than for a 30-year term. But for tax purposes, the 30-year term gives the borrower a higher tax deduction for the interest paid.

Of course, the shorter-term loan costs you $311.07 more each month, but don't forget that you'll enjoy the satisfaction of owning your home, free and clear, in half the time it takes with the 30-year mortgage.

Therefore, if you're looking for faster equity buildup and a way to save on interest charges, and you don't need the greater interest tax deduction of the 30-year, the 15-year could be the most sensible choice for you.

Figures 4.4 and 4.5 illustrate monthly payments (principal and interest) at selected interest rates required to amortize (pay off) 15-year and 30-year fixed-rate mortgages. To calculate your loan payment, at the top of the table row, select the appropriate rate of interest. The entry in that column where your interest rate and the loan amount intersect is the computed monthly payment (rounded to the nearest dollar) for principal and interest that you will pay to fully amortize the loan. Note that if your particular loan amount is not illustrated, you can simply add smaller amounts to calculate the payment you need. For example, with a loan amount of $110,000, add together the payments for a $60,000 loan and a $50,000 loan.

Special Types of Financing

Besides the standard ways of financing real estate, you also have a choice of special forms of financing. In certain cases, for example, especially when there's a lot of equity in the property, the seller can also be the lender.

Purchase-Money Mortgages

A *purchase-money mortgage* is a form of seller financing for which, instead of accepting cash for their equity in the property, the seller carries back a mortgage from the buyer.

Suppose, for instance, you buy a house for $110,000 with a $10,000 down payment, and you assume an existing $60,000 loan. The seller could

Figure 4.4 15-Year Fixed-Rate Monthly Payment (P&I) at Selected Rates

	Interest Rate, %										
Amount	5.0	5.5	6.0	6.5	7.0	7.5	8.0	8.5	9.0	10.0	11.0
$ 50,000	395	409	422	436	449	464	478	492	507	537	568
60,000	474	490	506	523	539	556	573	591	609	645	682
70,000	554	572	591	610	629	649	669	689	710	752	796
80,000	632	654	675	697	719	742	765	788	811	860	909
90,000	712	735	759	784	809	834	860	886	913	967	1023
100,000	791	817	844	871	899	927	956	985	1014	1075	1137

Figure 4.5 30-Year Fixed Monthly Payment (P&I) at Selected Rates

	Interest Rate, %										
Amount	5.0	5.5	6.0	6.5	7.0	7.5	8.0	8.5	9.0	10.0	11.0
$ 50,000	268	284	300	316	333	350	367	384	402	439	476
60,000	322	341	360	379	399	420	440	461	483	527	571
70,000	376	397	420	442	466	489	514	538	563	614	667
80,000	429	454	480	506	532	559	587	615	644	702	762
90,000	483	511	540	569	599	629	660	692	724	790	857
100,000	537	568	600	632	665	699	734	769	805	878	952

carry back the balance remaining, $40,000 in this case, in the form of a purchase-money mortgage payable under terms you negotiate with the seller. In this example, $40,000 represents the seller's equity in the property.

Purchase-money mortgages are an integral part of profitable realty investing. They're profitable because seller financing can usually be negotiated at below-market interest rates, and they can be made assumable. That means if you ever decide to sell the property that has assumable financing, you can earn money by financing ("wrapping") the assumable loan at a higher rate of interest.

Wraparound Mortgages

The *wraparound* is a second mortgage granted by the seller to a buyer, but the buyer only makes one loan payment. It's commonly used in tight credit markets when the seller has existing low-interest financing on the property and can use it to his or her advantage. The seller would "wrap" the existing loan with a new wraparound loan. The seller continues making payments on the existing loan while the buyer makes payments to the seller on the new wraparound loan. Since the wraparound usually has a higher rate of interest than the underlying loan, the seller earns a profit on the spread in interest rates.

Note: Be wary of wrapping a nonassumable mortgage. Nonassumable mortgages have certain clauses in their contracts, such as a *due-on-sale* or *acceleration clause,* that allow the lender to exercise a right to call on monies due and payable within 30 days if the property is sold or the loan is assumed.

Land Contracts

A *land contract*—sometimes referred to as an *installment contract, contract of sale, conditional sales contract,* or *agreement of sale*—is a contract strictly between buyer and seller without the involvement of a financial intermediary such as a bank. Under a land contract, a buyer agrees to purchase a property and pay principal and interest to the seller along with an optional down payment. Title to the property remains with the seller until conditions of the land contract are fulfilled. The buyer retains possession of the property; however, if the buyer should default on

Landlord Tale

In 1987 I found a great property in Las Vegas that, at first glance, appeared impossible to purchase with a small down payment. And it didn't seem likely that the seller would carry back any financing. This particular property was a custom-built 2,200-square-foot ranch on a half-acre, and the seller had it for sale at $119,000 with a $25,000 down payment. It had an existing 8 percent first loan of $40,000, and the listing agent doubted the seller would be willing to carry back a mortgage.

Not deterred, I made an offer of $92,000: I would pay $10,000 down and assume the existing first loan of $40,000, and the seller would carry back a second mortgage at 9 percent for the balance of $42,000. Neither my Realtor nor the seller's agent believed this offer had a one-in-a-hundred chance of being accepted. But to everyone's surprise, the seller made a counteroffer at $96,000, while accepting all the financial terms of my original offer. The only difference in the counteroffer from my original offer was a $4,000 increase in selling price, which meant the purchase-money mortgage would be $46,000. I gladly accepted the counteroffer.

Six months later I sold that property on installment for $115,000. We made the deal with a wraparound mortgage at 11.5 percent, and I ended up with a $5,000 cash down payment and netting $350 a month for the next 15 years. The reason it became so profitable was the underlying low-interest loans, which I continued to pay on while the buyer was paying me at the higher 11.5 percent rate. (You have to keep in mind that in 1987, 8 and 9 percent loans were cheap compared to the market-rate 10.5 percent new mortgages available at that time.) Finally, in 1992 the buyer took out a new mortgage, paid off the underlying loans, and paid me off.

Based on my experience, you never really know whether a seller will carry back a purchase-money mortgage unless you try by making a legitimate offer.

the agreement (not pay as agreed), the property would revert to the seller and the buyer would lose all principal paid.

As are wraparound mortgages, land contracts are useful in "wrapping" existing low-interest financing and earning a profit on the differential. The contract should stipulate that the buyer pays a certain fixed rate of interest, which to be profitable must be higher than the combined rates on the underlying loans.

Unlike a mortgage, in which the buyer of real property receives title to the property at closing, under a land contract the buyer does not receive title until all the required payments stipulated in the contract are made. And since the buyer does not have legal title to the property until it's fully paid for, this method is generally only practical when the seller provides all the financing because it would be difficult for the buyer to obtain additional financing from another lender. In other words, it would be difficult for another lender to use the property as collateral for a loan (place a lien against it) when the buyer does not have legal title to the property.

The two primary reasons an owner of real estate would offer seller financing are that it makes the property more salable, and it's a great opportunity to earn interest income instead of being cashed out in the sale.

Loan Assumptions

Instead of originating new financing from primary lenders, often you can simply take over someone else's existing mortgage and earn a huge amount of savings doing it. When you assume a nonqualifying loan, you usually don't have to pay for an appraisal, a credit report, or loan origination fees. All you pay is a low-cost assumption fee.

When you assume a loan, you take over the legal obligation to make the loan payments, and the lender releases the previous borrower from the liability. Again, many mortgages contain a clause that prohibits assumption, such as a *due-on-sale clause* or *acceleration clause.* Either one of these written stipulations in the mortgage contract make the loan due and payable within 30 days if the encumbered property is sold or the mortgage assumed.

Noteworthy

FHA loans originated before December 1, 1986, and VA loans originated before March 1, 1988, are completely assumable with no questions asked. However, both types of these loans that originated after the specified dates require that special qualifications be met before they can be assumed by the new borrower.

Loan assumption can be either with or without qualification. Note that FHA and VA loans originated before a specified date—December 1, 1986, the FHA and March 1, 1988, for the VA—can be assumed without qualification. This means all that's required is payment of a low-cost assumption fee, and no questions are asked of the borrower making the assumption. FHA and VA loans originated after these dates can still be assumed; however, qualification of the assuming borrower is required.

Adjustable-rate mortgages can usually be assumed too, although the assuming borrower is required to qualify. Traditional fixed-rate mortgages from conventional lenders are usually *not* assumable.

Six-Month Rollover, 100 Percent Financed

Figure 4.6 illustrates a creative financing technique that's based on the theory that a cash purchase commands a bargain price and that the seller is highly motivated to sell. This particular method involves paying borrowed cash for improved real estate, quickly renovating it, then flipping it (performing a fast sale) at a profit. Immediately after the sale, you pay back the borrowed money.

For example, suppose you have located a property that, if purchased for $67,000 cash and renovated, could be sold within six months for $100,000. And prior to the purchase you have arranged to have a lender who will lend you $72,000 for six months. Figure 4.6 illustrates how the numbers work.

For the purchase described in Figure 4.6, you would need a line of credit with a lender that will give you a personal loan for at least $72,000.

Figure 4.6 Six-Month Rollover, 100 Percent Financed

Purchase price		$67,000
Plus the following expenses to acquire and renovate:		
Closing costs	$ 500	
Cost to renovate	5,000	
Cost to finance	7,920	
Taxes and insurance (6 months)	300	
Utilities (6 months)	200	
Total expenses		13,920
Total expenses and cost to purchase		80,920
Selling price		100,000
Less the following selling expenses:		
Sales commission	6,000	
Closing costs	500	
Total expenses and cost to purchase	80,920	
Total overall expense		87,420
Net profit before taxes		$12,580

Or if you were fortunate enough to possess enough ready cash to use the six-month rollover technique without borrowing the required working capital, then you'd be that much further ahead because you would save $7,920 in finance charges.

The key to this investment strategy, assuming the working capital is to be borrowed, is to have a lender prepared to lend you the necessary money at a moment's notice. Then, once you locate a property you wish to invest in, because you're not tied to a lender and a mortgage on the property and all the cumbersome things that go with it—appraisal, credit check, etc., that take a lot of time—you can quickly negotiate a deal and cash the seller out.

Rule of thumb. To profit from this innovative method, you must apply certain guidelines, and only certain properties are appropriate. The rule of thumb is that, if you can buy the property for no more than two-thirds of its selling price after it's renovated, you have made a good deal. For instance, in the example in Figure 4.6, the purchase

Tip

When you purchase a property and intend to sell it within a year or less, you can earn substantial savings on title insurance. Most title companies will allow you to pay an additional retainer, usually $50, which will be the total cost of title insurance when you sell. The cost of such a policy without the retainer usually exceeds $500, so you can save $450 or more by paying in advance for the retainer when you purchase the property.

price is $67,000, which is two-thirds the selling price of $100,000. If you purchased a home for $80,000, after renovating it, the selling price would have to be at least $120,000 to meet the two-thirds rule of thumb.

Properties that best qualify for this method are those in which the sellers have a substantial amount of equity and are unwilling to carry back a note and that have *curable defects*—problems that can be easily renovated, such as cleaning and new paint—yet are sound in structure and overall construction. A substantial amount of equity means the sellers have, in most cases, owned the property for an extended period. Since they bought the property for substantially less many years ago and they are unwilling to carry a note or renovate the property, they would be inclined to sell at a bargain price in order to be totally cashed out of the property.

Home-Equity Loans

A *home-equity loan*, also known as a *take-out second loan* (as opposed to your *first mortgage loan*), is originated against your equity in the property. Say, for example, you have $60,000 equity in your home. You could take out a home-equity loan—usually for up to 80 percent of the equity in the property, which in this case is $48,000—to make renovations, pay off credit-card balances, pay for the kid's college education, or buy additional income property.

Tip

Home-equity loans can be good, but they are not for everyone.

Adjustable loans, as I mentioned before, make sense only for buyers who expect to repay the loan quickly (in less than three years). Remember too that the interest rate will increase (along with the monthly payment) if the Fed raises interest rates.

Buyers with long-term needs should always use fixed-rate loans.

Getting a home-equity line and mortgage from the same lender will often save money for the buyer. Since the buyer is already a good customer, the lender is likely to cut the buyer a break on the rate or fees. However, it often pays to shop around before signing on the dotted line. Rates on home-equity lines of credit can vary by as much as two points, and the loan origination fees from different lenders can vary widely also. If a lender is offering a low initial teaser rate, buyers should be sure to inquire how long that rate lasts and what the final rate will be after the teaser expires.

Unlike auto loans and credit-card loans, home-equity loans *are* tax deductible.

Refinancing versus a Home-Equity Loan

Often, after you've owned a home for several years and earned a substantial amount of equity and want to convert it to cash without selling the home, you are faced with a key decision—how to borrow against that equity. Essentially you have to decide between taking out a home-equity loan or refinancing the existing loan(s). The decision should be dependent on the interest rate you're already paying on the first loan and how it compares to the going market rate for first-mortgage loans. The home-equity loan is better only if the existing first loan has a below-market rate of interest. This way you create a new second mortgage and retain the existing low-interest mortgage.

Refinancing is better when market rates for first mortgages are substantially below the rate you're already paying on your existing first mortgage.

Rule of thumb. Refinance your existing mortgage when the market rate for new first mortgages is at least 2 points below the rate on your first mortgage and you intend to retain the property for more than two years. Why? Because the up-front costs to refinance—origination fee, appraisal, and credit report—can be substantial, say, $2,100. Then, if your monthly savings to refinance are $100 per month, it will take, in this case, at least 21 months to make up for the added cost to refinance.

Maximize Leverage with Special Loan Programs for Owner-Occupants

Before you can learn how to run, you first have to know how to walk. In other words, if you've never bought real estate before, buying a house is a good start. If you already own a home, a good choice as your next investment could be a larger home (and you would rent out the home you're living in) or a small four-unit apartment house. The following are some investment strategies along with a list of various high-leverage loan programs available to assist low-money-down investors.

If you don't already own a home, you can easily start investing in income properties. But first, it's important you keep this in mind: In order to qualify for owner-occupied financing, you have to honor the lender's occupancy requirement, which means you must intend to live in the mortgaged property for at least one year. With that stipulation in mind, you can begin the wealth-building process by selecting a high loan-to-value (LTV) loan program that's most appropriate for you.

Purchase a one- to four-family property, move in to it for one year, then rent it out, and repeat the strategy again. Even after you move out, the owner-occupied financing remains with the property.

Programs Available with No-Down- or Low-Down-Payment Possibilities

The following are nine programs that provide investors with all types of no-down- or low-down-payment possibilities:

1. *FHA 203(b).* This is the most popular program available through the Federal Housing Administration (FHA), which insures real estate loans through conventional lenders. Under this program cash-short

buyers can finance one to four units with as little as 3 percent down. Currently loan limits are $333,700 on single units, $427,150 on two-family units, $516,300 on three-family units, and $641,650 on four-family units. Qualifying standards are more lenient than they are for conventional loans, and loan applicants who show steady income and good faith in paying their bills usually qualify.

2. *FHA/VA 203(v).* This program is similar to the 203(b) except that it's offered only to qualified veterans and the down payment requirement is less.
3. *FHA 203(k).* This plan is ideal for home buyers who want to renovate, rehab, or add more value to a property. This two-in-one program allows you to combine a home's purchase price and renovation costs all in one mortgage.
4. *FHA qualifying assumptions.* When market interest rates are high, look for sellers with FHA mortgages originated when rates were lower. Pay the sellers for their equity (or whatever amount you negotiate) and then assume the seller's mortgage. Qualifying for this type of mortgage is a lot less complicated than originating a new loan, and you gain the benefit of acquiring a mortgage at below-market interest rates.
5. *FHA/VA nonqualifying assumptions.* Prior to the late 1980s, when the FHA and VA stopped making them, millions of these loans were originated. Though most of these loans have been repaid, a few sellers have retained them. The nonqualifying assumable loan is the easiest and least costly loan you can get. The reasons are that there are no questions asked of the borrower and all that's required is payment of a small assumption fee. See a list of repossessed VA-owned properties at their Web site, www.vahomeswash.com.
6. *HUD homes.* When FHA borrowers fail to make their loan payments, the Department of Housing and Urban Development (HUD), the parent of the FHA, takes over ownership of these properties. HUD properties can be purchased with as little as 3 percent down. For more details, ask a HUD-registered Realtor or see the HUD Web site at www.hud.gov.
7. *VA mortgages.* If you're an eligible veteran, you can borrow up to $240,000 with no money down to buy a home. To get the ball

rolling, remit your discharge papers to the VA to get your Certificate of Eligibility. No cash required to close and ease of qualifying are two more of the benefits given to those who served honorably in the U.S. military.

8. *VA qualifying assumptions.* Existing VA loans can easily be assumed by veterans or nonveterans. When market interest rates are high, look for sellers with VA mortgages that originated when rates were lower. And just like FHA no-qualifying assumptions, the VA loan is easy to qualify for and it costs less than originating a new loan would cost.
9. *Real estate owned (REO). REO* is a term that a commercial lender such as a bank or savings and loan uses to describe their inventory of foreclosed real estate. A large multibranch savings and loan, for example, would have an REO department that would oversee and manage its holdings. Should a lender foreclose on a house, for instance, the owner or tenant of the house would usually be evicted. Then the lender (who is now the new owner) would secure it and would eventually put it up for sale. More often than not, these properties are sold at bargain prices with great terms. Your job should be to make a thorough search of these REO managers in your area and get a list of their inventory. You could also find out who the Realtors are that make it their business to sell a lender's REO.

Loan Sources for Those with Poor Credit

If your credit history is not yet up to conventional standards and you're having difficulty finding a lender, there are less than conventional methods for securing financing. The following loans sources have less stringent qualifying requirements with the previously described options:

- *Mortgage brokers.* Because mortgage brokers are independent agents who often represent primary lenders nationwide, they're likely to know of lenders who arrange mortgage loans for buyers with less-than-perfect credit histories.
- *Nonqualifying assumable loans.* These, along with seller financing, are a great method of acquiring real estate, especially since the seller is likely not to be as concerned as a banker about your credit history.

- *Lease-purchase option.* You could find a seller who is willing to lease you the property and give you an option to purchase it. You could, for instance, negotiate a deal where you rent the property for $850 a month for three years. But in addition to paying rent, you pay an additional $250 a month in option fees that apply toward the purchase price. At the end of three years, you would have applied $9,000 (36 months × $250) toward the purchase price—the equivalent to a sizable down payment. An ideal subject property for a lease-purchase option is one that the seller owns free and clear of any loans. In this circumstance, there's no need for outside financing because the owner can handle the financing with a purchase-money mortgage or sell it to you on a land contract.
- *Cosigned loans.* With a cosigner on your mortgage loan, you have a better chance of qualifying for a mortgage loan with a primary lender. This method, however, makes the cosigner responsible for payment of the loan should you default.

Shopping for a Mortgage Loan

Earlier in the chapter you learned about the all-important interest rate—how you can save thousands of dollars over the term of a mortgage just by reducing the rate of interest on a long-term loan by 1 point. You can save more money by becoming familiar with points and other fees that mortgage lenders charge, along with how to compare loan offerings and where to shop for a mortgage loan.

Where to Start

The most common primary lenders for residential mortgage loans are savings and loan associations, banks, credit unions, and mortgage bankers. If you're already a customer of a bank, savings and loan, or credit union, start there. Established customers often can get preferred rates and terms.

Although not a primary lender, mortgage brokers can be helpful; they're independent agents in the business of "selling" loans, and they earn a commission for their services, which is paid by the lender. Brokers can be helpful in getting the best loan deal because they can shop among the many lenders they represent. And if your credit history is less than perfect and you're finding it difficult to qualify for a mortgage, a good mortgage broker can direct you to special lenders that may be willing to fund you a loan.

Points and Rates

When choosing a mortgage, you usually have the option of paying additional points—a portion of the interest that you pay at closing—in exchange for a lower interest rate. If you own the property for a long time—say, five years or more—it's usually more cost effective to take the points. The lower interest rate will save you more in the long run.

On the other hand, if you need to pay fewer points at the closing (due to cash constraints), you can pay a higher rate of interest. The shorter the term of the loan, the more sensible it would be to pay less up front and more later on.

Here's an example of the points–interest rate trade-off. Suppose that you want to borrow $120,000. One lender quotes you 7.5 percent on a 30-year fixed-rate loan with a 1-point origination fee. Another lender quotes 8 percent with no points. Which offer is better? The answer depends entirely on how long you intend to pay on the loan.

The 8.0 percent loan costs $880.52 per month.

The 7.5 percent loan costs $839.06 per month, plus 1 point, which is $1,200.

You save $41.46 a month with the 7.5 percent loan, but you have to pay $1,200 in points to get it.

To calculate which loan is more cost effective, divide the cost of the points by the monthly savings, which is $1,200 divided by $41.46 = 28.9. Therefore, it will take 28.9 months to recover the $1,200 cost of the points. So if you expect to pay on the loan for less than 29 months, then you would choose the no-points loan. But if you expect to pay on the loan for more than 29 months, selecting the 7.5 percent loan plus the 1 point will save you money.

The Annual Percentage Rate (APR)

When it comes time to compare loan offerings between lenders, compare *annual percentage rates* (APRs). It puts all the competitors on a level playing field. The APR is the true cost of credit offered to the consumer in percentage terms. Regulations in the Truth in Lending Act require that borrowers be fully informed of the cost of credit to allow a comparison of costs based on a uniform rate—the APR.

Before the enactment of Truth in Lending, a lender could have offered a consumer loan of $1,000, advertising a 6 percent rate of interest under a one-year term. But when the consumer applied for this loan, he or she was charged a $60 application fee, which was deducted from the loan proceeds, wherein the borrower only received $940. In doing so, the actual effective interest rate on borrowing $940 while paying back $1,000 was 6.38 percent, not the advertised 6 percent. This form of deceptive advertising is the reason why the Truth in Lending regulations came into existence.

The Loan Application Process

Before the lender will originate a mortgage loan, you'll have to complete a mortgage loan application. Prepare yourself for a huge paper chase because not only are you required to complete the application, you also must supply a vast amount of information—including W2s, divorce papers (if applicable), account numbers, and so on—and sign a lot of other documents, and it's very important that you leave no spaces blank. Just knowing what will be required of you is half the battle because it will help you to get organized in preparation for dotting all the i's and crossing all the t's.

It would be wise to get two copies of the loan application, take them home, and fill out the first one in pencil. When it's complete, transfer all the data neatly in pen to the final copy. This will be the copy you submit to the lender, neat and free of alterations and messy dabs of correction fluid.

On the loan application, be prepared to answer the following questions:

- Are you borrowing any part of the down payment?
- Are there any outstanding judgments against you?
- Have you ever been foreclosed on or given a deed in lieu of foreclosure?
- Are you obligated to pay alimony or child support?
- Are you a comaker or endorser on a note?

In addition, depending on your particular situation, you have to provide the lender with other information, which may include the following:

- *Proof of employment.* If you're self-employed, you'll need copies of federal income tax returns for the past two years. If not, you'll need recent pay stubs to verify your income.
- *List of assets.* This includes all your assets, such as cash in banks, stocks, bonds, CDs, and retirement accounts, along with all the appropriate account numbers and addresses.
- *Bankruptcy, judgments, and foreclosures.* If you experienced any of these in the past 10 years, you're required to report that information to the lender. (They will likely learn of it anyway in the credit report.)
- *VA documentation.* If the loan you're applying for is a VA-guaranteed loan, then you'll need to provide the lender with a Certificate of Eligibility. If you haven't already got one, it takes about a month to receive it from the VA after mailing in your proof of discharge, Form DD-214.

Get Preapproved before House Hunting

By getting preapproved for a mortgage loan, you'll save yourself the grief of looking at houses you can't afford, and you'll be in a better position to make a serious offer when you do find the right property. Not to be confused with *loan prequalification,* which is without lender verifications and is based solely on the cursory information the borrower provides, preapproval from a lender is based on verified documentation. Preapproval from a lender considers your actual income, liabilities, cash available, and credit history.

Loan-Underwriting Standards

Once the application is submitted, your loan request will be evaluated by the lender. To determine whether or not to approve the loan, primary lenders typically apply a variety of mortgage-underwriting guidelines. The more informed you are about these guidelines, the greater chance you have of finding a lender who will approve your loan request. And keep in mind that lenders always give their easiest and best credit terms to owner-occupants.

Besides loan-to-value ratios and occupancy requirements, the following are five other underwriting standards:

1. Capability (monthly income)
2. Collateral (the encumbered property)
3. The down payment
4. Credibility (creditworthiness)
5. Compensating factors

Capability (Monthly Income)

An important underwriting guideline is the borrower's capability to pay back the borrowed funds. To determine this, the lender will assess your monthly income from employment and other sources, along with (if applicable) the expected NOI of the property being financed. For loans on owner-occupied properties, lenders commonly use a housing payment-to-income ratio of 28 percent. In that case, the lender would limit your monthly mortgage payment (principal, interest, taxes, and insurance, or PITI) to 28 percent of your gross monthly income. For instance, with a housing payment-to-income ratio of 28 percent and gross monthly income is $3,500, the lender would limit your monthly payment (PITI) to $980.

With regard to rental property, the lender places a lot of emphasis on the property's ability to generate sufficient income to cover operating expenses and debt service. Many lenders apply a *debt coverage ratio* (DCR) to determine the maximum loan amount, including a certain amount of safety margin of income that exceeds the sum of operating expenses and debt service. The following is an example of a six-unit apartment building whose units rent for $800 a month:

Gross annual rent (6 × $800 × 12)		$ 57,600
Less:		
Vacancy and credit loss	2,880	
Operating expenses and maintenance	11,520	
Property taxes and insurance	4,032	
Total operating expenses	18,432	-18,432
Net operating income (NOI)		39,168

In the example given, should the lender require a 25 percent safety margin of income over debt service, the maximum allowable mortgage payment can be figured by dividing the property's NOI by a DCR of 1.25. Here's how the numbers work:

$$\frac{\text{(NOI) \$39,168}}{\text{(DCR) 1.25}} = \text{(annual mortgage payment) \$31,334}$$

Divide the annual mortgage of $31,334 by 12, and the result is a monthly mortgage payment of $2,611 utilizing a 1.25 DCR. To calculate the amortized-loan amount based on a mortgage payment of $2,611 a month over a 30-year term, see Figure 4.7.

For example, if interest rates were 6.5, 8.0, or 9.5 percent, typically the lender would limit the mortgage loan to the following amounts: At 6.5 percent, the limit would be $413,133; at 8.0 percent, the limit would be $355,722; and at 9.5 percent, the limit would be $310,464.

Here's how those loan amounts were calculated:

$$\frac{\text{Monthly mortgage payment: \$2,611}}{\text{Monthly payment per \$1,000 at 6.5\%: 6.32}} = \text{\$413,133 loan amount at 6.5\%}$$

$$\frac{\text{Monthly mortgage payment: \$2,611}}{\text{Monthly payment per \$1,000 at 8.0\%: 7.34}} = \text{\$355,722 loan amount at 8.0\%}$$

$$\frac{\text{Monthly mortgage payment: \$2,611}}{\text{Monthly payment per \$1,000 at 9.5\%: 8.41}} = \text{\$310,464 loan amount at 9.5\%}$$

Note that the higher rates of interest decrease the maximum amount you can borrow. Therefore, the interest rate and the debt coverage ratio are the two key factors in calculating the maximum you can borrow.

Figure 4.7 Monthly Fixed-Payment (P&I) Cost per $1,000 at Selected Interest Rates, Term 30 Years

Interest, %	Monthly Payment	Interest, %	Monthly Payment
4.0	$4.77	7.5	$ 6.99
4.5	5.07	8.0	7.34
5.0	5.37	8.5	7.69
5.5	5.67	9.0	8.05
6.0	5.99	9.5	8.41
6.5	6.32	10.0	8.77
7.0	6.65	10.5	9.15

Collateral (Encumbered Property)

Primary lenders have guidelines for properties that they will accept for collateral pledged against their mortgage loans. Many conservative lenders will finance only single-family dwellings. Others won't underwrite loans in declining or run-down neighborhoods. And some lenders won't finance properties larger than four units. Primary lenders may also set standards with regard to building regulations, paved streets, and proximity to schools, shopping, and public transportation.

Before choosing a particular lender, it would be wise to find out if the subject property you intend to buy meets the lender's collateral standards. Otherwise, you'll be wasting time completing the loan application and squandering money for the cost of such prepaid items as an appraisal and credit report.

The Down Payment

As another underwriting standard, lenders like to see their borrowers invest some of their own cash into their purchased properties at the time they buy them. How much they require depends on if it's considered investment property and/or a residence and if the property will be owner occupied. Typically, when the loan involves investment property, the lender sets the maximum loan-to-value (LTV) ratio at about 70 percent. However, the LTV may go higher, perhaps to 80 percent, if the property will be owner occupied. On noninvestment property, lenders commonly set a maximum LTV as high as 97 percent or more, depending on whether the loan has government backing and whether the property is owner occupied.

Primary lenders also want to know the source of the down payment. On the loan application you will be asked where you're getting the cash: Will it be from cashing in CDs, a savings account, or perhaps from the sale of common stock? Most of the time, lenders don't want to hear that you're borrowing the down payment from parents or taking a cash advance against your credit card.

Also regarding your liquid assets, lenders would like to see a certain cash reserve on hand after you take possession of the property. Preferably, they would like you to have at least three months' cash on hand (or near-cash assets) to cover three months of mortgage payments.

Credibility (Creditworthiness)

Good credit saves you money because primary lenders base their lending rates on the amount of risk they take underwriting a loan. The better your credit score, the less risk the lender needs to take, which correlates into the borrower's being charged a more reasonable rate of interest with better terms. Conversely, poor credit means the lender is more at risk, and it will result in the lender's charging much more for the loan. In fact, the lender could require more of a down payment; or worse, the lender could flat out disapprove the loan.

When it comes to investing in real estate, you need favorable interest rates and terms on the money you borrow because it's such a crucial function of optimizing your profits. If you don't already have good credit, you need to do all you can to establish or rectify your credit record and develop a good reputation for paying all your debt obligations on time.

If your credit history isn't what it should be, you have the opportunity to remedy it, even if you have experienced foreclosure, repossession, or bankruptcy. If in the past you have experienced any of these hardships, some mortgage lenders will still consider you for a loan. In order to qualify with these more lenient lenders, essentially you have to show worthiness in the following three areas: You must have good credit without any flaws for the past 18 months; you should be capable of attributing any poor credit to unemployment, divorce, accident, or other misfortune; and, you must convince the lender that you're now in complete control of your financial well-being and fully capable of paying back the loan.

Not long ago if you had serious credit problems, you had to wait five years, and sometimes longer, to qualify for a new mortgage. But the modern mortgage lending business is very competitive, and primary lenders today are more inclined to give capable people a second chance, especially if the intention is to live in the property they want to mortgage.

Compensating Factors

Remember that these are merely loan-underwriting guidelines, not commandments etched in stone. Most primary lenders allow a certain amount of flexibility in their decision making; in fact, under certain conditions a loan committee, rather than one person alone, makes the decision to approve a loan. And in doing so the committee weighs and considers all the factors concerning the borrower and the property. Due to such contemplation, you have the opportunity to positively influence the lender into approving your loan. You can enhance your positive attributes and give good explanations for any shortcomings.

A well-thought-out written business plan that shows the lender how you intend to renovate the property and increase net income would be helpful. If your credit history is flawed, compensate for it with pledged collateral or a larger down payment. If you've changed jobs often, emphasize how long that you've stayed in the same industry and that you have had several promotions with related increases in salary. If the lender is concerned about your inexperience in managing real estate, overcome this objection by informing him or her that you're educating yourself by reading instructional books on buying and managing real estate and that you've developed a profitable investment strategy as reflected in your written business plan.

Keep in mind too that lenders are different; they have differing standards. What one lender rejects, another will accept. Don't be afraid to make your loan request with several lenders. And finally, never give up on the loan you want because sooner or later, as long as your request is within reason, someone will give you a loan.

Chapter Lessons

- Always choose fixed-rate financing unless you intend to hold the property for less than three years, in which case, the choice of an adjustable-rate mortgage would be more cost effective.
- Refinance your existing mortgage loan when interest rates are at least 2 points below the rate you're already paying.
- Remember that to succeed and profit at realty investing, you must view the financing of real estate as a joint venture with your lenders. As an investor, however, you don't have to share with the lender the profits realized; you're required to pay them only the interest on your use of their money.
- Be wary of overextending yourself and having big expectations. I know of a man in Florida, who, expecting a 15 percent annual

appreciation, bought a fourplex for $250,000 with $25,000 down. Two years later, because the real estate market turned sour, he ended up losing his down payment plus 15 months of subsidizing his negative cash flow. The lessons here are the following:

1. Never expect the value of the property purchased to appreciate excessively.
2. Beware of negative cash flows.
3. Don't overpay.
4. Never overextend.

5

Selecting the Best Professionals to Help You

Key Points

- *Letting the Realtor be your guide*
- *Tips for hiring the best Realtor, contractor, home inspector, lender, accountant, escrow officer, and lawyer*

When it comes to investing in real estate, you will need to draw upon a lot of special expertise in areas you or your partners are not familiar with. For example, you might need to have a thorough home inspection conducted by a licensed inspector before you make an offer on a property. Or you might need the advice of a building contractor on the cost to renovate the kitchen. Or you might need help in reviewing the tax laws pertaining to your purchase, or you might need legal advice for the closing transactions. Whatever the situation, if you need to hire an expert in a particular field, you want to avoid someone who just occasionally dabbles in the real estate business, such as your neighbor's brother or your spouse's cousin. Instead, hire a full-time professional who earns a living in the real estate specialty you need.

Chapter 5

Tips for Hiring the Best Professionals in Their Fields of Expertise

To avoid making costly errors and achieve maximum success in buying a home or income property, you need specialized expertise of competent professionals to advise you. This includes real estate professionals who are full-time experts that can help you make wise decisions. Think of purchasing real estate as playing in a football game you want to win. Since you cannot play every position on the team, you assemble a group of competent players to play the other positions. And it's your job to lead the players in such a way that they can advise you on how to win the game.

The following is a brief look at the professionals you need as advisors:

- *Realtor*. A good full-time real estate agent will be familiar with local real estate values where you want to buy and will have your interests at heart when it comes to negotiating on your behalf, making sure that you don't overpay for the property.
- *Mortgage lender.* If you're like most home buyers and cannot pay all cash for a realty investment, you're going to require a loan. A good primary mortgage lender will offer a variety of competitively priced loans and can help you choose the best loan for your special needs.
- *Property inspector*. With a qualified property inspector to thoroughly check out what could be the largest purchase you ever make, you will be assured that you're not buying a lemon and that you're, in fact, getting precisely what you are paying for.
- *Contractor*. You need a building contractor who is licensed and has a proven work record in construction and renovations similar to your project, not a fly-by-night unlicensed guy who pretends to be what he's not.
- *Lawyer*. Depending on where you live in the United States, you may not need a lawyer for advice in purchasing real estate. In many regions of the country an independent escrow officer or a title company agent handles all the essentials at a real estate closing. But even if your state laws do not require it, if you have any doubts or questions about the legality of your purchase contract, be sure to consult with a lawyer who specializes in real estate law.

It's always better to use professionals who specialize full-time rather than part-time in their field of endeavor. Every deal has problems of one kind or another that will require the skill of a trained, experienced specialist. Also, remember that people who work only part-time may not be available when you need them.

Another good practice is to seek the advice of local people to the greatest extent possible. Local professionals will be well informed about the area and will have current information on any pending zoning changes or development plans that may be in the works. They will also likely have excellent connections with building contractors and other specialists who can help you.

Hire people based on their reputation and track record. The best way to find specialists in the field of real estate is to get referrals from satisfied customers. Keep an eye out for examples of work you admire. This can be the appeal of a property's landscape design or perhaps the remodeling work being done on a particular building. Then find out who the landscape designer or contractor was that did the work you appreciate. Also, become informed about competent local lawyers and accountants who have expertise in projects like yours. For example, if you have a zoning problem, it's important that you hire a local lawyer who is knowledgeable in zoning matters and has the political connections to get things accomplished.

The Realtor

A good Realtor can not only save you thousands of dollars in completing a deal but he or she can also tend to many of the details necessary to complete the purchase and usually make the entire process a hassle-free experience. On the other hand, a bad or inexperienced Realtor can cost you thousands and turn what should be a smoothly running procedure into a jittery nightmare.

Knowledgeable, well-versed Realtors serve their clients in several ways. They're helpful in finding the special type of property that meets their clients' particular needs. They can also help negotiate for the property on behalf of their clients, advise them on the financing (keeping their clients informed of the going market interest rate and referring their clients to a lender with low-cost financing), and coordinate the closing (act of sale).

The Realtor As Your Best Source of Information

Your experienced local Realtor is your best overall source of information. For instance, say you see a property that's beautifully landscaped and you want to know who the landscape designer was. Either the Realtor will have this information or he or she can find it for you.

How do you get the Realtor's cooperation? Explain the reason you need the information—that you, for instance, intend to buy a big two-story home on a corner lot along the city's growth corridor. Tell the Realtor that you intend to maintain it as a residential rental until an appropriate time, then convert it to a small office building.

The Realtor will likely be very enthusiastic about obtaining the information you need, especially if he or she thinks you're serious about buying a property. And you could entice the Realtor even more by letting it out that you presently don't have a Realtor and you need a competent one who knows the area you're interested in.

Realtors can network too with other specialists in the industry, and if they don't have the information you need, they can get it from someone else. Furthermore, an experienced Realtor will likely have a lot of valuable information stored in his or her database. He or she can reveal pertinent data about an exquisite building you're interested in. Such data might include who the most recent buyer was, the name of the lender and amount of the loan, what it cost to build, and the name of the contractors. If he or she doesn't have it in a database, he or she will know where to get it for you. And you're not limited to approaching just one Realtor. Contact two or three because some may be more willing to help you than others.

The Qualities of a Competent Realtor

A competent Realtor has certain qualities that give him or her a distinct advantage over the ordinary or sub-par Realtor:

- *The Realtor is not a part-timer working at another profession*. He or she is a full-time professional that will give you full-time effort. Unfortunately, many rookies that are newcomers to a real estate career work part-time on weekends and after normal business hours. That may be satisfactory for them but not for you.

- *He or she is a specialist in certain types of properties and geographic areas.* Like other professionals, Realtors too need to specialize in a specific type of property (such as residential or commercial), within a certain geographic boundary, so that they can concentrate their efforts and become more knowledgeable about specific areas. Realtors who try to work outside their areas of expertise or who endeavor to be all things to all their clients invariably deliver mediocre service.
- *He or she is an advisor, not a decision maker*. A competent agent will always advise you of all your available options and not make decisions for you. This way you can weigh the alternatives and in the end make a wise decision.
- *He or she has good contacts.* You're better served by a Realtor who has numerous working relationships with other specialists such as other Realtors, local lenders, property inspectors, insurance agents, and escrow or title companies. Realty investors feel comfortable doing business with skilled service providers who are highly recommended by others, who are trustworthy, and who offer competitive pricing.
- *He or she is well organized takes you on carefully planned tours.* A competent Realtor knows precisely what you're looking for and will have prepared a well-thought-out tour of properties to show you.
- *The Realtor is not too overburdened and has time to serve you.* Avoid Realtors that are too busy with many other customers because they won't have sufficient time to serve you adequately. If you ever feel neglected due to constraints on the Realtor, look for another to represent you.
- *He or she is an ethical person.* A principled Realtor will always alert buyers to problems with the condition or location of the property.

Where to Find Your Realtor

You can start by getting referrals. Get recommendations from neighbors, friends, or coworkers who have recently been involved with the purchase or sale of real estate. Seek referrals from professionals in related fields too such as architects, building contractors, or financial advisors because they will probably know who the outstanding Realtors are in your area. When you're out prospecting for properties, talk to Realtors who are holding open houses. These people could be ideally suited for your particular needs since you already know that they work in the community in which you want to buy.

Also, consider visiting a local real estate office in the region you're interested in. Look around the office for performance awards and ask to meet with some of these top performers. This way you avoid the dabbling part-timer.

The Buyer's Agent

Instead of representing both buyers and sellers, which has been the norm for Realtors over the years, nowadays there are also "buyer's agents" who will represent only the buyer in a real estate transaction. Buyer's agents can be helpful when they represent you in a for-sale-by-owner (FSBO) situation. Often the commission for this kind of service can vary, depending on how much work is involved. You can usually negotiate with the FSBO sellers so they will pay at least half the buyer's agent's fee.

Never get involved with a buyer's agent who insists on charging you a fee up front for his or her services just for finding the property you want to purchase. Buyers should never be expected to pay a commission in advance to get a buyer's agent to work for them.

Simplifying the Prospecting Process

It's essential that the Realtor knows ahead of time, before you go out prospecting, precisely what it is you're looking for. This includes the price range, architectural style (such as ranch or French colonial), number of bedrooms and baths, lot size, approximate square footage, and location preferences. You also want to limit viewing to no more than six to eight properties per day. Looking at too many properties in one session can be confusing and fatigue your mind. Also, take along a camera and make notes. Allow the Realtor to drive so you're free to take notes, ask questions, and make observations.

The Mortgage Lender

As previously mentioned, the most expensive thing you'll likely ever buy is not your house—it's the cost of the financing to acquire the house. That said, with so much at stake, you need a top-notch primary lender to do business with. A good place to start looking for a lender is the bank, savings and loan, or credit union with which you already do business. If there's no one there you want to work with, talk to your Realtor about who is making mortgage loans in the area you want to invest in. The experience and knowledgeability of the lender is important to ensure that you get a loan that allows you to prepay it without penalty.

The Property Inspector

Since you never want to end up with a real estate lemon—a property with all kinds of expensive hidden problems—you need the assistance of a qualified property inspector. A property inspector can ease many uncertainties and can uncover costly problems and save you thousands of dollars on the price of the property. A professional home inspector licensed by the American Society of Home Inspectors (ASHI) charges about $250, depending on location. Once you've found a home that you're interested in buying, be sure to make the offer contingent upon your approval of a home inspection conducted by an independent contractor.

Two things you never want to do when hiring a home inspector: Never hire the inspector that the seller recommends, and never use the Realtor's recommendation either. Using the seller's referral is not a good idea because the interests of the seller's inspector will conflict with your interests. The seller doesn't want the inspector to find anything wrong, and that could influence the inspector's objectivity. And the reason you don't want a Realtor's referral is that even the most competent property inspector might avoid making too many waves for fear that the sale will fall through. If the Realtor loses a sale because the property inspector finds too many faults in the home, the Realtor might never recommend the inspector again.

So how do you go about finding a competent home inspector? Get referrals from friends or business associates who have recently used an inspector. Also check the Yellow Pages of your local phone book under "building inspection services" or "home inspection services."

Before you hire a property inspector, you should first conduct a simple phone interview with several of them. The following are good questions to ask:

- *Are you a full-time professional property inspector?* You don't want a part-time dabbler.
- *How many property inspections do you perform each year?* An active inspector will perform 100 to 250 inspections a year. It's important that the inspector you hire be familiar with the area where the property to be inspected is located, to ensure that the inspector is familiar with local codes, local building regulations, and local problems (such as mud slides, floods, tornadoes, or earth quakes).
- *Do you carry insurance for errors or omissions?* Errors-and-omissions insurance protects the homeowner should the property inspector make an error or overlook a problem.
- *Are you licensed or certified?* Qualified property inspectors usually have experience in some related field such as construction, engineering, or electrical work. Membership in the ASHI or other professional associations for property inspectors indicates some knowledge of property inspection procedures.
- *How thorough is the property inspection?* Check that the inspection covers all the property's major mechanical and structural components from the foundation to the roof. Never accept anything less.
- *What type of inspection report do I get?* You need a detailed written description of the property's mechanical and structural condition. It has to be written in plain English, and it must fully explain the implications of the inspection.

For the name of a home inspector in your area, contact:

American Society of Home Inspectors
932 Lee Street, Suite 101
Des Plaines, IL 60016
(847) 759-2820
(800) 743-ASHI
www.ashi.com

The Contractor

Contractors build their businesses based on their reputation for dependability and the quality of the work they perform.

When you hire contractors,

- Be sure they are licensed and bonded and that they employ union labor if necessary.
- Check their references.
- Find out how long they have been in business.
- Find out if they will be available at the time you want the work done and if they have the number of employees they will need to do the job.
- Check with the Better Business Bureau to see if there are any complaints against them.
- Check their place of business. If it's dirty and unkempt, their work may be sloppy too.
- If possible, try to negotiate a fixed-price contract.
- Find out when they can start the work and when they will be finished.
- Get everything in writing.

The Lawyer

The purchase agreement you sign is a legally binding contract between you and the seller. Should you have any doubts about the legality of your contract, consult with a local lawyer who is well-versed in real estate law.

The following factors determine whether you should hire a lawyer:

- *Location of the property being bought or sold.* In the state of Mississippi, lawyers (instead of escrow companies) handle everything from preparing the purchase agreements to the closing (act of sale). In other states, however, private escrow companies do everything required for a closing and/or act of sale, and rarely is a lawyer involved. Your Realtor will know whether a lawyer is needed in your sate.
- *Complexity of the transaction.* Whenever you get involved in a complicated deal or have anything extraordinary about your purchase, you need a lawyer experienced in real estate law. Complexity usually arises in partnership agreements, intricate leases, or thorny titles.

- *Absence of a Realtor.* If you're involved with the purchase of a property being offered directly by the owner, it would be advisable to have a lawyer prepare the purchase agreement and do the work the Realtor would normally handle. When no Realtor is involved, you still should have advice on negotiations, contingency clauses, the property inspection, the financing, and other important details in the purchase procedure.

When you decide that you need a lawyer, remember that law is a very specialized field. With that in mind, it would *not* be wise to hire your cousin's divorce lawyer or your brother in-law who is celebrated as a great corporate attorney. On the contrary. You need to get referrals and hire a recommended lawyer from your community who specializes in real estate law. A good place to get referrals is your Realtor. He or she probably has good working relationships with lawyers in your area.

A good competent lawyer has the following qualifications and abilities:

- He or she is licensed to practice law in your state and works full-time solely in the legal profession.
- He or she has local expertise. Since real estate law not only varies from state to state but also from one region to another within a state, it's smart to have a competent local lawyer represent you because he or she will know the law in your area.
- He or she speaks your language.

The completion of a profitable and trouble-free deal is no accident; it's a very thoughtful coordination of a group of skilled professionals. Each professional blends his or her contributions with the thoughts of the decision maker, who weighs all the alternatives presented and makes the final decisions based on the coordinated efforts of everyone involved in the transaction.

6

The Sources

Where to Find Bargain-Priced Realty

Key Sources

- *Newspaper advertisements*
- *Realtors*
- *FSBOs*
- *Internet shopping*
- *HUD repossessions*
- *VA repossessions*
- *Federal government auctions*
- *Sheriffs' sales*
- *Lenders' real-estate-owned properties*
- *Private auctions*
- *Delinquent-tax auctions*

If bargain-priced real estate were readily available for anyone to buy, every breathing sole over the age of 21 with the slightest bit of ambition would be trying to buy it. Since it's not, you need the knowledge of where to look for it and the perseverance to find it. And when you do find it, you need to negotiate its purchase.

Besides looking for bargain-priced real estate that's available for purchase through Realtor listings, you also have a broad source of properties among those that are for sale by their owners (FSBOs) as well as those that are for sale through special auctions, HUD repossessions, and other types of foreclosure sales.

Newspaper Advertisements

Search the classified sections of your local newspaper under the column "Real Estate for Sale." When you find an interesting offer, circle it with a pen. After you have accumulated an ample supply of interesting ads, cut each one out of the paper and staple it to the left-hand margin of an 8.5- by 11-inch piece of plain paper. Now you have adequate space to make notes about the property advertised, and the larger paper can more easily be filed in a file folder or in a three-ring binder than the smaller cut-out advertisement.

Begin calling the phone numbers on the cut-out ads. Make queries about available owner financing and down payment requirements. Ask about square footage, lot size, architectural style, condition and age of the property, and reason for selling. Try to get as much information as you can, and make notes on the ad sheet. Then, if the property still sounds promising, make an appointment with the Realtor (if the ad is a Realtor's ad, it usually will be specified as such) or the owner.

Realtors

To effectively work with Realtors, you need to supply them with precise information about what you're looking for. If, for instance, you're looking for a house for yourself, the specifics you would give the Realtor should include the architectural style you prefer, the number of bedrooms and bathrooms, approximate square footage, area of town you wish to live in, the price range you can afford, the amount of down payment you can afford, and condition of the property (such as a fixer-upper or relatively new construction). Also inform the Realtor that you want to know if owner financing is possible or if the owner will permit FHA and (if applicable) VA financing.

A Realtor has a source of listed properties derived from a Multiple Listing Service (MLS) book that covers every property listed for sale with Realtors in a certain area and that is usually published every other week. The MLS book is a great tool for investors to gather information from. Once you develop a working relationship with a Realtor, ask him or her to lend you last week's MLS book so that you can study the listings. Once you have access to the MLS book, carefully go through it noting properties of special interest. On another 8.5- by 11-inch sheet of paper, note the property address and the MLS page number. Then later when you call or drive by the property, you can make notes on the reference sheet.

While you're studying the MLS book, take note of important information that's usually listed in the back. Often you'll find recent sales prices of past listed properties. This is valuable information that will help you get a feel for values in the local market. Try to establish an average square-foot selling price, which will later come in handy when you have to quickly estimate market value of a potential acquisition.

FSBOs

As mentioned earlier, the FSBO is a property that's for sale by its owners. The owners are obviously trying to sell their property without the assistance of a Realtor for the purpose of saving the cost of a sales commission, which is about 6 percent of the sales price. Frequently, these FSBO sellers find themselves at a terrible disadvantage when they realize they neither have the exposures of the Multiple Listing Service nor the professional services of many Realtors seeking buyers for their property. Many FSBOs fail to find a buyer, and in time they eventually list their property with a Realtor, realizing that the sales commission ends up being money well spent when they get the assistance they need to finally sell the property.

If you find an FSBO and are interested in purchasing the property, it would be good advice to seek professional help regarding the use of purchase agreements and seller disclosures. Consult with an experienced local Realtor or lawyer for assistance in getting the property under contract and following it through all the normal procedures to closing.

Also, if you've been working with a Realtor and find a particular FSBO of interest, show your loyalty and have the Realtor contact the FSBO. Then if the seller is unwilling to pay your Realtor a commission, you should pay it. Normally a 3 percent commission would be an equitable fee because that is the amount the listing agent would have earned under a typical listing agreement.

Internet Shopping

Nowadays real estate investors surf the Internet for bargains. Thousands of real estate–related Web sites now list properties for sale. Internet subscribers can access the Realtors' Multiple Listing Service at www.realtor.com.

You will also find a growing industry of network providers who provide specialized listings of everything from FSBOs to foreclosed properties. Virtually all the real estate–related information is now on the Web that once was available only from newspaper ads, Realtors, and public records.

The following Web sites listed according to category should prove useful.

City and Neighborhood Data

- Research the features of a particular community with www.homestore.com, where you will also find a page called "The School Report," which provides information about every public school district in he United States.
- The Department of Commerce, Bureau of Economic Analysis (BEA), Web site www.bea.doc.gov also provides state and local economic data, ideal for reviewing information about the economic health of a particular community.

Comparable Sales

- www.dataquick.com
- www.propertyview.com

Credit Information

- www.creditaccuracy.com
- www.creditinfocenter.com

Foreclosures and Repossessions

- www.brucebates.com
- www.all-foreclosure.com
- www.va.gov
- www.bankhomes.net

Home Improvement

- www.hometime.com
- www.askbuild.com

Home Inspection

- www.ashi.com is the site of the American Society of Home Inspectors. It provides a list of certified home inspectors and information about the home inspection process.
- www.creia.com

Insurance Information

- www.fema.gov is the site of the Federal Emergency Management Agency. It shows where various disasters (such as tornadoes, earthquakes, and floods) are apt to strike. It also supplies useful educational resources on such topics as flood insurance and disaster preparation and prevention.
- www.cpcu.com
- www.statefarm.com

Legal Information

- www.lectlaw.com
- www.lexis.com

Mortgage Lenders

- www.eloan.com offers an array of mortgage loans from a wide variety of lenders, along with handy tools for comparing the cost of different loans.
- www.interest.com
- www.hsh.com
- www.homepath.com

Real Estate Listings

- www.realtor.com is a comprehensive site sponsored by the National Association of Realtors (NAR).
- www.hud.gov lists repossessed properties with HUD and other government agencies.
- www.vahomeswash.com is a national list of repossessed VA-owned properties.

Important: Never accept any Web-based data as the last word. Verify all information with at least one back-up source. When making appraisals, physically view comparable sales, visit schools, and check out neighborhoods.

HUD Repossessions

When FHA-insured borrowers fail to make their loan payments, the primary lender forecloses and places the property up for public sale. If the property does not sell, the lender turns in an insurance claim to HUD (Department of Housing and Urban Development). Then HUD reimburses the lender what is owed, and HUD takes over ownership of the foreclosed property. Finally, HUD puts the property, along with all the others it recently acquired, on the market for public sale.

HUD repos can be a great source of potential bargains for you as a potential investor, but you have to consider some important shortcomings. HUD properties are sold "as is," without warranty. That means the buyer, not HUD, will have to correct all problems with the purchased property. The other disadvantage is that repossessed properties, more often than not, have been seriously neglected over the years. Owners usually defer maintenance first before they allow their mortgage payments to become delinquent. Therefore, you can expect at least a couple of years of deferred maintenance on most repossessed properties.

However, even if a HUD property needs fixing up—and not all of them do—it can still be a great buy. For instance, HUD's asking price will usually reflect the fact that the buyer will have to make improvements. Also, HUD might offer special incentives, such as allowances to upgrade the property or cover moving expenses, or a bonus for closing early. And on most sales, the buyer can request that HUD pay all or a portion of the closing costs. Your participating HUD Realtor will have details. Be sure to have a HUD property professionally inspected before you make an offer so that you know what repairs will be needed.

Finding HUD Properties

You can locate HUD property in several ways, including cruising the neighborhoods searching for HUD's for-sale signs, browsing the local newspaper for HUD's weekly ads, or visiting HUD's Web site at www.hud.gov.

Owner-Occupants' Priority

HUD favors owner-occupants over investors in two ways: First, owner-occupants have first choice, and second, they are offered FHA low or nothing-down insured financing. Recently, the FHA has begun refusing to offer investors FHA insurance on HUD properties.

The owner-occupied edge. During the first five days the property is on the market, HUD will accept bids only from buyers who intend to occupy the premises. If the property remains unsold, HUD will then allow anyone to bid for the next five days, but the owner-occupied bidders have the edge. The investor can win the bid only if no prospective owner-occupant submits an offer, even if the investor submits the highest bid. Only during the third selling round will HUD not give an advantage to buyer status.

Owner-occupant certification. HUD enforces stiff penalties to discourage investors from falsely claiming owner-occupant status. All owner-occupied buyers are required to sign a purchase contract addendum that certifies that they will occupy the property as their primary residence for a minimum of 12 months. Also, all Realtors who submit owner-occupants' bids must sign a certification that they're not knowingly representing an investor. Penalties for false certification are as high as $250,000 fine and two years in federal prison.

Purchasing HUD Property

Only HUD participating Realtors are permitted to sell HUD property, and they must submit your bid for you. Normally, HUD properties are sold during an *offer period.* Upon expiration of the offer period, all offers are opened, and the highest reasonable bid is accepted. If a particular property goes unsold during the offer period, you can continue to submit bids until it's sold. Bids can be submitted any day of the week, including weekends and holidays. Bids are opened the next business day, and if your bid is accepted, your Realtor will be notified within 48 hours.

Should HUD accept your bid, your Realtor will help you through the paperwork process. HUD will issue a settlement date, usually within 30 to 60 days, by which time you need to arrange financing and close the sale. If you cannot close by then, you will forfeit your earnest-money deposit or pay for an extension of your sales contract.

For more detailed information, contact a participating HUD Realtor, or check out HUD's Web site at www.hud.gov.

VA Repossessions

Similar to HUD repos, the VA (Veterans' Administration) takes back unsold foreclosed properties from primary lenders that the VA guaranteed the loans on. The properties are then offered for sale to the public.

Selling Procedures

(Note that most VA rules and procedure are similar to those of HUD.)

- Bidders are required to submit their bids through a VA-approved Realtor. (No negotiations directly with the VA are permitted).
- VA properties are sold through a sealed-bid process. Bidders can submit multiple bids either as owner-occupants or as investors.
- The VA sells all its properties strictly as is, without any warranties whatsoever.
- The VA charges buyers who select its financing a 2.25 percent guarantee fee.
- The VA guarantees marketable title, and it allows buyers to obtain a title policy.
- The VA accepts bids only on VA forms and documents.
- The VA advertises its properties through a combination of broker lists, newspaper ads, and Internet Web sites such as www.va.gov.
- A 1 percent earnest-money deposit of the purchase price is required to be held on all VA properties. All earnest-money deposits are made payable to and held by the Realtor unless otherwise directed by the

VA. If you're the successful bidder, the earnest money will be immediately deposited in the Realtor's escrow account; otherwise, it will be directly refunded.

- The VA may decide to keep the earnest-money deposit if a bidder fails to close a successful bid for any reason other than failure to obtain financing.
- Similar to HUD purchase contracts, the VA does not allow a contingency for a property inspection after submitting a bid. However, bidders are allowed to inspect a VA property prior to making the bid.
- Buyers receive a vacant property at closing. The VA, when necessary, will evict homeowners or holdover tenants prior to listing a property for sale.

Advantages for Investors

Although the VA and HUD have similar procedures, the VA has two distinct rules that favor investors:

- *Unlike HUD, VA owner-occupant bidders do not receive preferential treatment over investors*. The VA accepts the bid that results in the highest net proceeds regardless of the bidder's buying status.
- *Financing that the VA offers is very advantageous*. Usually a person can buy a VA property with less than 6 percent of the selling price total out-of-pocket cost. And the VA has qualifying standards that are more lenient than HUD's.

For an online listing of VA-repossessed property, see www.va.gov. Keep in mind that you do not need to be a veteran to purchase a VA repo and that anyone is eligible to obtain VA financing on any property purchased.

Other than great financing with lenient terms, many investors find the VA repo program attractive for the following reasons:

- VA financing is assumable, which makes the property easier to sell because the buyer can take over the existing VA loan. During periods of tight credit (high mortgage interest), a low-interest assumable loan becomes very attractive.
- Since you'll have a small amount invested with corresponding high leverage, you should earn an accelerated return on investment as long as you paid a bargain price for the property.

- Even when you end up paying near market value for a VA repo, within a year such high-leveraged properties should rent for enough to provide at least a breakeven cash flow situation.

Federal Government Auctions

Other than HUD and VA repossessions, each year the federal government auctions off all types of surplus and seized real estate, including homes, apartment buildings, office buildings, multiacre estates, and vacant land. The most active sellers at these auctions are the Internal Revenue Service, the Federal Deposit Insurance Corporation, and the General Services Administration.

Each of these organizations maintains a list of available properties, along with rules and procedures for buying them, at the following Web sites:

- Internal Revenue Service, www.gov/auctions/irs
- Federal Deposit Insurance Corporation, www.fdic.gov/buying/owned/real/index
- General Services Administration, www.propertydisposal.gsa.gov

Sheriff's Sales

A *sheriff's sale* (or *judicial sale*) is a legally forced sale that results from a foreclosure, property tax lien, a civil lawsuit judgment, or a bankruptcy proceeding.

For instance, if property owners go beyond a certain stage of delinquency on their mortgage loan, they are notified by the lender and the circuit court of the county that they can redeem their delinquency by remitting the overdue mortgage payments, along with any due penalties. If the owners do not pay, they are then considered in default of the loan, which will result in the mortgaged property going to a sheriff's sale. Conducted by order of the circuit court, these sales are usually held in a designated municipal building, or in a title company office.

Property sold at a sheriff's sale is sold strictly as is. Buyers are required to have a cashier's check for 10 percent of the sales price of the property being purchased. The balance owing has to be paid within 24 hours of the sale. Usually, the sale has to be confirmed in front of a circuit judge within four weeks of the sale, which allows the owners in default one last chance to redeem the property. This reprieve, of course, means that the buyer does not legally own it until the judge confirms the sale.

It would be a good idea to attend a couple of sheriff's sales before you become an active participant. This way you will get a feel for how they are conducted before bidding in a similar circumstance yourself. You have to be wary of assuming other obligations (such as delinquent taxes or other liens attached to the property) when you buy. So it's likely you'll need to do a title search before you buy at a sheriff's sale.

Lenders' Real-Estate–Owned Properties

Real estate owned (REO) is foreclosed real estate that has failed to sell at public action. It now belongs to the primary lender who made the mortgage loan and used the property as collateral against the loan. Large financial institutions usually manage their REO out of their corporate headquarters.

An REO is usually sold through a designated Realtor.

An REO can be a great source of bargain-priced real estate for the following reasons:

- You can often get the seller, who is also a primary lender, to arrange a low-cost mortgage loan with a small down payment.
- You can usually negotiate to have the seller pay all closing costs.
- The property is usually clear of any liens because they were likely eradicated during the foreclosure sale.

Anyone interested in purchasing a lender's REO should call the REO department of a large primary lender and find out who is responsible for selling it. Then get a list of the available property through them.

Private Auctions

During poor economic times sellers often decide to liquidate their properties through private auctions. During the early 1990s in California a large group of bankers pooled their REO properties, and they jointly auctioned off hundreds of properties at a time. And frequently, especially during typical slow periods of the year, housing developers will liquidate their closeout inventory with a public auction, so afterward they can devote their time and effort to the next housing project. And at other times, a home builder in financial difficulty will use an auction to stimulate home sales in order to fend off his or her creditors.

Where to Find Auctions

Most auctioneers advertise the event in local newspapers, and large-scale auctions you'll occasionally see in national media, such as large display ads in the *Wall Street Journal.* Notably, part of their marketing strategy is to add the names of those who register to their mailing list. Auction companies strive not only to attract the maximum number of prospective buyers but also to attract big crowds so they can instill a festive mood of excitement and anxious anticipation.

Also look for list of local auctioneers in the Yellow Pages. Names of nationally known auction companies who hold large-scale local auctions include Hudson and Marshall, J. P. King, NRC Auctions, and Ross Dove and Company.

Auction Preparation

If you're interested in buying at an auction, it's advisable that you first attend one just for the experience—not to buy. It's interesting to see how they operate—the professional auctioneers and bidders contending with each other.

The following are steps you should take in order to prepare for an auction:

- *Always have an established maximum bid price in mind*. Avoid getting caught up in the frenzied atmosphere that auctioneers like to create. Keep thinking about your established maximum bid price, remembering that the further below your maximum you can buy it at, the better the bargain. Never allow the auctioneer's boosters bamboozle you into overbidding.
- *Before you bid, thoroughly inspect the property*. Prior to the actual sale, auctioneers schedule open houses for potential bidders to look over the inventory. Auction property will often sell at dirt-cheap prices because they're dilapidated old buildings waiting to be torn down.

Or they may suffer from incurable defects. You or your inspector need to always thoroughly inspect property at an auction before you offer a bid.

- *Carefully appraise the property*. Compare the subject property to at least three similar comparables in the same neighborhood. Never rely on list prices. The only way you avoid overpaying is having knowledge of property values in your area of interest.
- *Study the related paperwork*. Prior to the auction, ask to see documents that pertain to the subject property—the lot survey, the property tax assessment, the legal description, and the purchase contact you'll be required to sign.
- *Have an adequate deposit*. Eligible bidders are required to register before the auction begins and show proof of adequate funds (typically a cashier's check for 10 percent of the successful bid price is common). Registrants are then issued bid cards making them authorized bidders. Unauthorized bids made by people without bid cards are not accepted.
- *Find out what type of deed you'll get*. Under a *warranty deed*, the seller guarantees clear title, subject to certain exceptions. Other kinds of deeds transfer fewer warranties. Before you accept a deed, be sure of its limitations, such as encroachments, easements, or recorded liens. Your best protection is to buy title insurance. And if for any reason the property's title is uninsurable, get an opinion from a competent real estate lawyer.
- *Learn all the details of the sale*. Make inquiries about the financing available. Auction companies will often have prearranged financing on some or all of their properties. If so, get the details of the terms and what it takes to qualify. If you must provide the financing, find out how much time you're allowed to do so. Private auctions differ from government agency auctions in that payment in cash is not required. And inquire about whether the action will be held under *absolute terms* or subject to a *reserve price*. There is no minimum bid requirement under absolute terms. Under terms of a reserve price, the highest bid must exceed a prearranged minimum price, or the property is removed from sale.

Chapter 6

Delinquent-Tax Auctions

In Sarasota, Florida, Manatee County has an annual *tax certificate auction* held on the tenth floor of the County Administration center in downtown Sarasota. On the first day the auction is held, it's not uncommon for the deputy tax collector and several other county employees to preside over the auction of more than 10,000 certificates for delinquent taxes on real estate. Here's how it works.

When real estate owners don't pay taxes on their property, the county issues certificates for the amount of the unpaid taxes. The certificates are auctioned to investors for the amount of the unpaid taxes, plus a small processing fee. When property owners pay the taxes, they must also pay the certificate holder interest at a rate set at the auction, usually limited to a maximum of 18 percent.

If the property owners neglect to pay the taxes within two years, certificate holders can petition the county to sell the property at auction. Certificate holders recoup their investment, including interest, from the proceeds of the sale.

Some auction participants are hoping the taxes will be paid so they can collect the interest with minimum hassle. But other participants want the property, not the interest. If the taxes go unpaid for two years, the certificate holder can fill out the appropriate paperwork, pay about $200, and ask the county that the property be sold. The sale would be advertised and an auction held if the taxes are still unpaid. The certificate holder will assume ownership if no one bids for the property.

Risk involved. Such ventures can be risky if you don't do your homework before bidding. The certificates expire after seven years. This means certificate holders will lose their investment if they fail to petition the county to auction the property before the certificates expire.

Investors also risk holding certificates for property that's virtually worthless—such as platted lots in old subdivisions that were never developed. It's better to look for properties in developed subdivisions, particularly waterfront property.

Besides all these great bargain potentials, there are other bargain opportunities lurking right around the corner: they're just not as obvious.

The Sources

Great bargain opportunities can be found just by cruising the neighborhood. Get your camera and notebook out and start driving up and down the streets in your area noting listed properties as well as FSBOs. While you're at it, keep an eye out for property likely to be for sale but which has no for-sale sign. Telltale indications are unkempt vacant properties, boarded-up houses, and homes that are in dire need of care.

Once you have a substantial list, you can obtain ownership records from your local county courthouse or the property tax collector's office.

7

Appraisals

Finding the Right Property at the Right Price

Key Points

- *Defining market value*
- *The three methods of appraisal*

What you pay for real estate is just as crucial to optimizing your profits as the financing that goes with it. In this chapter I have addressed the three primary methods of appraisal the professionals use. By carefully reviewing them, you should be able to make accurate appraisals on your own, and they should assist you in learning how to spot a bargain. Knowing how to accurately evaluate real estate serves another important purpose too—it reduces the risk of overpaying when you buy!

Defining Market Value

What is *market value*? It can mean different things to different people. To inexperienced investors, language such as *sales price*, *appraised value*, and *market value* all have the same meaning. But they're as different as day and night. *Appraised value* could be associated with an estate tax appraisal, an insurance appraisal, a property tax appraisal, or a market value appraisal. *Sales price* is precisely that: it's the nominal price the property sold at. The sales price of a property can be equivalent to, or be substantially greater or lesser than, the market value. In order for sales price and market value to be equal, the for-sale property has to meet the following criteria:

- Both buyers and sellers are fully informed of the market and all related circumstances.
- No favorable or special terms of financing are involved.
- The property has had a reasonable period of marketing exposure to potential buyers.
- There are no extraordinary concessions being offered by either the sellers or buyers.
- Neither the sellers nor the buyers are acting under duress.

Here are several examples of how extraordinary situations can distort values. Say you found two comparable properties that are similar and in the same area as the property you're interested in. Property A sold for $179,000, and property B sold for $175,000. Both comparables have about 1,650 square feet of living area, are relatively new, and are in good condition. The nearby house you're interested in is similar in size and amenities and priced at $149,900. At first, it appears that you may have found a bargain. But before you jump to any quick conclusions, you have to be wary of the criteria the comparables were sold under.

What if the buyers of property A, after selling their small home in Beverly Hills for $700,000, drove to Biloxi, Mississippi, and bought the first home they saw because it was "the greatest bargain they ever saw"? Property A actually cost only one-fifth of their Beverly Hill's home, but remarkably it had more modern features and twice the square footage. This situation is a good example of uniformed buyers; they were not familiar with the Biloxi real estate market.

What if the sellers of property B gave the buyers a nothing-down, 5 percent, 30-year mortgage when market interest rates were averaging 6 percent? This situation is a good example of special financing. And notably, the differential between 5 and 6 percent interest on a loan of $175,000 is worth about $108,000 in savings over 30 years.

Just knowing what other properties have sold for is not sufficient information when you're bargain hunting for properties. Erroneous or incomplete sales price information clouds the true market value of a property. Before you evaluate a particular subject property, always verify the accuracy of your information. In other words, you must find out whether the buyers and sellers were fully informed of market conditions, accepted any unusually favorable seller financing, sold (or bought) in a hurry under duress, and/or made any concessions that could have, either way, influenced the sales price. If you do learn that the reported information from comparable sale properties does not meet the definition that warrants a market value sale, carefully evaluate that information before making any offers.

The Three Methods of Appraisal

A professional appraiser or a knowledgeable investor will typically evaluate improved real estate using the three different methods listed below. The appraiser arrives at a final opinion on the value of a given subject property by weighing the different results obtained from each of these methods:

1. *Reproduction cost*. With this method of appraisal,(also referred to as *replacement cost appraisal)* the appraiser considers how much it would cost to build a subject property at today's prices. The appraiser then deducts an appropriate depreciation allowance of the improvements and then adds the depreciated cost figure to the current value of the land.
2. *Comparable sales*. Using this approach to valuation, the appraiser compares the subject property to other similar (comparable) properties that have recently sold in the same area. The appraiser then adjusts the price of the subject property according to the prices of certain amenities that differ among the similar properties—such as the square footage, location, or quality of construction—either positively or negatively to arrive at a market value figure.

3. *Income capitalization.* With this method, the appraiser analyzes the net operating income of a property. The appraiser then "capitalizes" the NOI according to a predetermined rate of return to arrive at a fair market value for the subject property.

Reproduction Cost Appraisals

This method is ideally suited for unique residential properties, such as expensive custom-built homes, when suitable comparables are not available to compare the subject property to. It evaluates a property in three steps: First, it takes today's cost of replacing all improvements that have been made on the property since it was last sold. Second, it deducts a depreciation allowance to determine the present market value of the improvements. Then it adds the depreciated market value of the improvements to the value of the land.

Calculating the Cost to Replace the Improvements

As shown in Figure 7.1, the first step in reproduction cost appraisals is to figure what it would cost to build the improvements using dollars per square foot. Costs per square foot of residential construction vary throughout the country so if you are using this appraisal method, use a cost estimate that's based on the costs of construction in your area. To learn these square-footage costs of construction, consult with a local building contractor or review construction cost manuals in the reference section of your local library.

Deducting the Depreciation of the Improvements

Once you've calculated the cost to replace the improvements, you have to deduct an amount for two types of depreciation: physical and functional. Over time a building ages and becomes less desirable than newer buildings because of wear and tear. As the years pass, the building starts to slowly deteriorate the more it is exposed to the weather and the longer it is used by its occupants. Gradually the frayed carpets, cracked walls, and leaky roofs reduce a building's value when compared to new construction.

How much you allocate for this *physical* depreciation is a tough decision. Typically, for a building that is not too old and is in good condition, 10 to 15 percent physical depreciation is a fair estimate. For an older run-

Figure 7.1 Replacement Cost Appraisal

Item	Cost
Dwelling (2,000-square-foot living area × $72)	$144,000
Upgrades	7,000
In-ground pool and sprinklers	15,000
Garage (500 square feet × $22)	11,000
Total cost of improvements	177,000
Less: Physical depreciation (10%)	−17,700
Functional depreciation (5%)	−8,850
Total cost of improvements less depreciation	150,450
Site improvements (landscaping and driveway)	8,500
Land value	40,000
Indicated market value, replacement cost approach	$198,950

down building, an allowance of 50 percent or more could be appropriate. Another, possibly easier, way of allotting a percentage for physical depreciation is to calculate the entire cost of renovations necessary to restore the building to good condition.

An allowance for *functional* depreciation is made by computing the loss of value through obsolescence. Over time a building's function can become outdated because of such things as an underpowered electrical system or a poor architectural plan. The end result is that the property loses desirability because it lacks the modern features that appeal to the majority of would-be renters and buyers.

Adding the Land Value

The last item in the replacement cost evaluation is the estimated value of the land the improvements are situated on.

Comparable Sales Appraisals

Also commonly referred to as *market data appraisals,* this method is appropriate for evaluating detached single-family homes, condominiums, co-ops, and small apartment houses (up to four units) when a number of similar properties are available for comparison. In contrast, this method would not be appropriate for appraising a unique 4,200-square-foot custom-built home because it would be difficult to find similar comparables in the same area.

Start by finding three comparable properties that have recently sold (within six months) in the same area and that closely match the subject property. The comparables should match in approximate size, age, condition, amenities, quality of construction, floor plan, and room count.

Now look at the following two appraisals: the first is a quick appraisal based only on square footage, and the second looks at both square footage and the feature of the properties. Both appraisals take into consideration the price per square feet of living area, but the second is more precise because it also compares the subject property to the comparables on a feature-by-feature basis.

Quick Appraisal Based Only on Square Footage

Suppose you have located three comparables for the subject property. Comp A has 1,620 square feet, Comp B has 1,730 square feet, and Comp C has 1,885 square feet. Each of these homes has sold within the last four months for the respective prices of $115,020, $111,325, and $130,442. To determine the selling price per square foot of living area, you divide the square footage of each home into the selling price:

$$\text{Comp A:} \quad \frac{\$115{,}020}{1{,}620 \text{ square feet}} = \$71 \text{ per square foot}$$

$$\text{Comp B:} \quad \frac{\$111{,}325}{1{,}730 \text{ square feet}} = \$64.35 \text{ per square foot}$$

$$\text{Comp C:} \quad \frac{\$130{,}442}{1{,}885 \text{ square feet}} = \$69.20 \text{ per square foot}$$

If the subject property you're appraising has 1,810 square feet of living area, then based on comparable square-footage cost, calculated from an average of the three comparables of $68.18, you can quickly determine that its estimated market value is approximately $123,400.

Determining market value based only the square footage of comparable sales will suffice when you need a quick, off-the-cuff estimate. However, to make a more exact evaluation, you also need to compare the subject property to the comparables on a feature-to-feature basis.

Appraisal Based on Features and Square Footage

Once you have the three comparables, you have to adjust for differences in features and amenities between them and the subject property. You accomplish this by adding or subtracting the value of features to and from each comparable to make them equivalent to the subject property. In effect, you want to know what the comparable would have sold for had it been precisely (with the same features) like the subject property.

For example, looking at Figure 7.2, consider the –$4,000 adjustment to Comp B for sales concessions. The $111,325 sales price in the deal included the seller's custom-made draperies. Since draperies are not usually included in a real property sale, the sales price had to be adjusted down to make it equal in value to that of the subject property, whose sale does not include this particular item.

The following are more explanations for several other adjustments listed in Figure 7.2:

- *Comp A, financing concessions at –$4,000.* This comparable had valuable seller financing in the form of a low-interest purchase-money mortgage at 7.5 percent with only 5 percent down. Since at the time of the sale, the market interest rates were 8.5 percent with 20 percent down, the value of favorable owner financing must be deducted from the sales price.

Figure 7.2 Adjustment Process

Item	Comp A	Comp B	Comp C
Sales price	$115,020	$111,325	$130,442
Features:			
Sales concessions	0	–4,000	0
Financing concessions	–4,000	0	0
Date of sale	0	2,000	0
Location	0	0	–10,000
Floor plan	0	3,000	0
Garage	5,000	0	8,000
Pool, deck, patio	–4,000	0	–6,000
Indicated value of subject	112,020	112,325	122,442

- *Comp A, garage at +$5,000.* The subject property has an attached two-car garage while Comp A has only a single-car garage. To equalize the difference, you have to add $5,000 to Comp A's sales price. (If Comp A had been constructed with a two-car garage, it would presently be worth $5,000 more.)
- *Comp C, location at –$10,000.* Unlike the subject property, Comp C has a great location at the end of a cul-de-sac with a wonderful view of a nearby lake. Thus, the added value of a great location with a view has to be deducted from the comparable to equalize the value of the subject property.

At this point you might ask the question, how do I arrive at an exact dollar amount for each of these features? There is no easy answer. However, as you gain expertise at evaluating real estate, you begin to get a feel for what certain things are worth. Meanwhile, when you're out prospecting for bargains, don't be afraid to ask a lot of questions. Ask your Realtor about construction costs and lot values. In particular, keep informed about costs per square foot of living area, based on different qualities of construction. As you're viewing different properties, make a list of features that make a difference. Ask the Realtor or a building contractor what he or she thinks the added feature is worth. Then weigh their evaluations against your judgment to arrive at a value for a particular feature.

Income Capitalization Appraisals

Often referred to as the *income approach* to appraisal, this method analyzes the net operating income (NOI) of the subject property, then divides it by a suitable rate of return to arrive at a fair market value.

To determine the property's NOI, start with the gross annual income at 100 percent occupancy, then deduct all operating expenses, including allowances for vacancies, credit loss, and replacement reserves. The resulting NOI then has to be capitalized at a specified rate of return. To calculate market value with the capitalization approach, use the following formula:

$$V \quad \text{(value)} = \frac{\text{NOI}}{R \quad \text{(rate of return)}}$$

V is the estimated market value, NOI is the net operating income of the property being evaluated, and *R* is rate of return on capital that investors of similar properties would typically expect.

Net Operating Income

The *net operating income* (NOI) is basically what the property would earn after all operating expenses were deducted from the property's gross annual income. This figure represents what the property would earn if purchased for all cash, free and clear of any loans. Figure 7.3 is what an income statement would look like for an 18-unit apartment house in which each unit rented for $575 a month.

Figure 7.3 Income Statement (Annual)

1. Gross annual rent ($575 × 18 × 12)		$ 124,200
2. Other income (laundry: $360 × 12)		4,320
3. Less vacancy and credit loss (5%)	$ 6,210	
Less the following operating expenses:		
4. Trash removal	480	
5. Property taxes	18,000	
6. Insurance	4,200	
7. Utilities	5,220	
8. Business license	35	
9. Advertising	480	
10. Management	7,800	
11. Reserve for replacement	6,210	
12. Supplies	240	
13. Total operating expenses including vacancy and credit loss	48,875	– 48,875
14. Net operating income		79,645
15. Less loan payments (P&I)		– 62,200
16. Gross spendable income (cash flow)		17,445
17. Principal payment (equity buildup)		4,200
18. Gross equity income		21,645
19. Less depreciation		– 21,200
20. Real estate taxable income		$ 445

The following list explains each numbered item in the income statement in Figure 7.3:

1. *Gross annual rent.* This is the total annual rent the property would earn at 100 percent occupancy.
2. *Other income.* This line is reserved for additional income other than rent.
3. *Vacancy and credit loss.* The national average for vacancy rates is 5 percent of gross rental income. Better neighborhoods can be as low as 3 percent, and bad crime-ridden areas as high as 10 percent.
4. *Trash removal.* This is the total annual cost to remove trash from the property.
5. *Property taxes.* This is the actual real property tax bill for the current year.
6. *Insurance.* This item represents the total annual cost of premiums for all necessary forms of insurance. If the insurance is included in a blanket policy that covers several properties, then you would allocate a proportionate expense for each property.
7. *Utilities.* This is the cost for a full year's operation, including gas, water, and electricity.
8. *Business license.* Certain municipalities require a business license to operate apartment buildings. Use the actual cost for the entire year of operation.
9. *Advertising.* This item represents the total annual cost of newspaper advertising along with the cost to make rental signs for the property.
10. *Management.* The total cost of employing the resident manager goes on this line. If you use the services of a management company, that cost can also be included.
11. *Reserve for replacement.* This item covers a budgeted reserve fund for all repairs and replacement of special capital equipment. These items include furniture, draperies, blinds, carpet, and equipment such as elevators, water heaters, air-conditioners, and so on. A fair estimate is 5 percent of the gross annual income.

12. *Supplies.* Rental forms, cleaning supplies, and all miscellaneous items are included in this category.
13. *Total operating expenses.* A summation of all operating expenses before debt service. As a rule of thumb, annual operating expenses as a percentage of gross annual rent should be in the range of 37 to 51 percent, with 40 percent being the average.
14. *Net operating income.* This figure is the result of deducting the total operating expenses from the gross annual rental income. It represents what the property would earn if it were purchased for all cash, free and clear of any loans. This item is also used to determine the capitalized value by dividing it by an appropriate rate of return.
15. *Loan payments.* This is the debt service of principal and interest paid on the loans.
16. *Gross spendable income.* This figure is the result of deducting the annual debt service from the NOI, or the actual cash (cash flow) that you'll have remaining after paying the property's expenses and debt service.
17. *Principal payment.* This item refers to the principal portion of the loan payment. It is also the equity buildup that you earn as you pay down the loan.
18. *Gross equity income.* This figure results from adding annual equity payments to the gross spendable income.
19. *Depreciation.* As a rule, about 80 percent of the property's cost can be depreciated for income tax purposes; the remaining 20 percent is allocated to the land, which cannot be depreciated.
20. *Real estate taxable income.* This figure results from deducting depreciation from the gross equity income. It's also the amount reported to the IRS.

When you figure the property's NOI, be sure to include all expenses for the coming year. Be wary of inaccuracies on the seller's income statement. Sellers tend to understate or omit expenses and overstate income in an attempt paint a rosy picture. Even if the seller is perfectly honest in reporting last year's income and expenses, it's your responsibility to determine how each of these line items should be adjusted up or down in future years. Remember that you're *not* investing in the past or present; you're investing in the future.

Note whether the seller has included a sufficient allocation toward reserve replacement and vacancy and credit loss. These are two line items that are often understated. Other items need careful inspection too. Has the seller deferred maintenance on the property? And has the seller self-managed the property and therefore neglected listing this item as a management expense? Never accept anyone else's income statement without verifying the accuracy of every line item.

Determining a Suitable Capitalization Rate (*R*)

Once you've calculated the NOI, you have to make a decision about what rate of return (capitalization rate) to use to convert the property's earned income into market value. The rate of return on invested capital is called *capitalization,* or *cap rate.* It is defined as the rate of return—expressed as a percentage—that's considered reasonable to expect for certain kinds of investment. The riskier the investment, the higher the rate of return the investor would expect. Typically, the investor usually selects a cap rate within the 8 to 14 percent range by considering the risk of the investment, the type of property, and the quality of the income.

Say, for example, you're considering buying a rental property in a high-risk area (high-crime slum neighborhood). You would expect a high rate of return on the investment. Thus, a high cap rate of 12 to 14 percent would be selected. If, on the other hand, you intend to invest in a low-risk prime area of town, where you could expect a better grade of tenant and a high rate of appreciation on the property, you would consider a lower rate of return, such as a cap rate of 8 percent. For rental property in an average part of town, you would choose an in-between cap rate of 10 to 11 percent.

Based on an average cap rate of 10 percent and an NOI of $79,645 (see item 14 in Figure 7.3), the result is a value of $796,450. Take note of what happens to the value when different cap rates of 8 and 12 percent are applied to the same amount of NOI.

Use the basic formula to determine the value:

$$V = \frac{\text{NOI}}{R}$$

$$V = \frac{\$79{,}645}{0.12} = \$663{,}708$$

$$V = \frac{\$79{,}645}{0.08} = \$995{,}562$$

Note the inverse relationship between rate of return and value. The value increases as the rate of return decreases. Rental property investors are not just purchasing a *quantity* of income. They pay for *quality* too. They also pay for anticipated appreciation potential. Consequently, the lower the quality of the income flow, along with less anticipated appreciation, the higher the cap rate. Or the opposite is applicable—the higher the quality of the property's income and potential for appreciation, the lower the cap rate.

Since most realty investors would prefer owning a rental property in a prime, growing area, as opposed to a crime-ridden declining area, they typically are more inclined to pay significantly more for the income earned by such a property.

To illustrate this principle, consider two four-unit apartment buildings. One property was recently constructed and is situated in a nice neighborhood with close proximity to shopping, quality schools, and entertainment. The other is 15 years old and located in a deteriorating part of town where some businesses have closed, properties are not properly maintained, and crime is on the rise. Given that each of the four-unit apartment buildings had yearly NOIs, respectively, of $24,220 and $12,110, how much do you think a typical informed investor would pay for each property?

In most cases, the typical investor would apply different cap rates to each property because of so many differences in quality between the two. The newer, better-located property has the potential for steady rental income, greater appreciation, and less neighborhood risk. You would likely see the newer, better-located property with a cap rate of 8 percent, while the older property situated in a deteriorated area capitalized at 14 percent. Here's how those numbers work:

$$\frac{\$24{,}220\ (\text{NOI})}{0.08\ (R)} = \$302{,}750\ (V)$$

$$\frac{\$12{,}110\ (\text{NOI})}{0.14\ (R)} = \$86{,}500\ (V)$$

The Final Estimate of Market Value

As mentioned earlier, "market value" differs from "appraised value" and "selling price." In order for sales price and market value to be equal, the property has to be sold under certain criteria. When using the comparable sales approach, you have to investigate the terms and conditions under which the comparatives were bought.

Although you can use the three approaches to estimate the market value, usually all three do not result in the same value. You have to decide which approach best suits the subject property. For instance, if you intend to appraise an owner-occupied house, the income approach would not be suitable (no income). But all three methods of appraisal would be appropriate for a four-unit apartment building because you have income and comparables, and you can figure the replacement cost.

Keep in mind too that the accuracy of an appraisal directly relates to how well you describe the features of the subject property and the comparables. To be able to put this accurate data into your appraisals, you must know square-footage costs of construction, features, neighborhoods, and lot values.

When you have made your appraisal using the three methods described, in the final analysis, your estimate of fair market value is said to be "within an indicated range of value," such as $124,000 to $129,000.

Chapter Summary

Most of the market information that appraisers gather is from secondhand sources (Realtors, lenders, public records, etc.). For example, appraisers seldom see the interiors of the comparables used in their market analysis reports. When information is only secondhand and unverified, the evaluation is often faulty. Therefore, accept a professionally prepared appraisal with a grain of salt, and never give it more weight than it deserves. You always want to verify the appraiser's data before accepting his or her evaluation as being accurate.

Finally, when you do find information about comparables that does not meet market value criteria, use this new information to help you in negotiations. During negotiations it's very likely that the seller will try to justify his or her selling price by showing so-called accurate comparables. If you can exploit the fact that the comparables are overpriced because of special conditions not reported in the appraisal, such as special financing concessions or uninformed buyers, you may be able to convince the seller to substantially lower his or her expectations.

For more negotiation tactics and principles for real estate, please turn to the next chapter.

8

Negotiations

Principles and High-Powered Tactics for Real Estate

Key Points

- *Principles of negotiation*
- *Negotiation tactics*
- *Structuring the purchase contract*

Principles of Negotiation

According to George H. Ross, executive business and senior legal advisor to Donald Trump, and costar of the hit television show *The Apprentice,* "The ability to negotiate intelligently is the key to the completion of any successful real estate transaction, large or small. It's mastering preparation, knowledge of human nature, learning how to uncover and exploit weaknesses, learning special skills, and many other intricacies. Good real estate negotiation principles are developed with the aim of getting others to agree with your ideas" (from *Trump Strategies for Real Estate: Billionaire Lessons for the Small Investor,* Wiley, New York, 2005).

Trying to influence other people to your way of thinking is what negotiation is all about. If you can adopt some of the negotiation principles and tactics portrayed in this chapter, you will give yourself a big advantage over the other side.

Find Common Interests That Can Precede the Negotiation

It's always a good idea to open negotiations with some chitchat rather than jumping right in talking about the price you're willing to pay. Think of it as a warm-up before you get down to business. You never want to initiate a competitive spirit or portray a winner-take-all attitude about the negotiation.

You could, for example, find a common theme while you're in their office. Look for family pictures or sports memorabilia and ask questions about them. "Are those your children?" Or, "Do you have grandchildren too?" In another situation, you might see that they're Chicago Cubs fans. In that case you could inquire about how the Cubs are doing this season, especially without Sammy Sosa. And if you're not familiar with the Cubs organization, you could learn about them and be prepared to chitchat about them at your next meeting.

Don't Be Misled by the "Look of Legitimacy"

The *look of legitimacy* is the tendency of people to believe things they see in print or they hear spoken by the media or some other apparently authoritative source. It affects the decision-making capability of those who are misled by its influence. Here are some examples of how it works:

I am shopping for carpets at a national home improvement store, and I intend to spend about $1,000. I make an inquiry with a sales associate and ask him, if I make a considerable high-quantity purchase, could a discount be arranged? The associate replies to my inquiry by saying, "We already have the lowest retail prices and never give discounts."

Then, about a month later, I'm at the same store, and I intend to buy a large amount of building materials that day. So I ask for the store manager and tell him that I'm building a house and that I intend to spend about $800 on drywall, drywall mud, and lumber, and I would like a volume discount. His reply is, yes, he can give me a discount but only on the drywall supplies. After the discount, I end up saving $124 on my total bill.

If I had listened to the sales associate's earlier claim of "no discounts," the bill would have cost me $124 more than it did! In other words, I was lead to believe through a look of legitimacy that there were no discounts.

A real estate advertisement by a major Realtor specified a home for sale at a price of "$249,000 firm." The word *firm* was inserted into the advertisement to make the reader believe that the price was not negotiable, so that a potential buyer would make an offer close to the so-called nonnegotiable asking price. A friend came to me for advice because he was unsure of what to offer on the home, which sounded like a property he had to have.

I said, "What were you planning to offer?"

"Well, it's a great property, and the seller did say $249,000 firm, so I was thinking of offering $235,000."

I told him, "You're putting too much on the table. Offer $150,000."

He shook his head and replied, "He won't even give me a counteroffer with such a lowball figure like that! I'll lose the deal to someone else."

I said, "You'll never know unless you try. Why don't you give it a shot?"

He finally took my advice, and three weeks later he bought the house for $179,000. He was almost misled by the look of legitimacy—in this particular deal, to the tune of $56,000!

Shrewd real estate investors refuse to accept the look of legitimacy as if it were gospel etched in stone. You cannot accept everything you read or hear from sellers, Realtors, or experts or everything you see on television as if it were precise, unflawed information. For example, say, you're interested in a particular property, but the seller seems to be asking an excessive price of $290,000. You start asking questions, and the seller's agent says, "Well, the property has been appraised at $300,000." The look of legitimacy here is someone's appraisal, which you must keep in mind is only one person's opinion of value.

Plan Your Negotiations

A researcher named Ziff made a study of negotiation from which he developed a concept called *Ziff's principle of least effort*. His research proved that most people will put forth the least amount of effort necessary to conclude a transaction. This principle correlates perfectly with the advantage a prepared negotiator has over his or her unprepared adversary. Entering into negotiations without preplanning is a huge and often costly mistake.

Most people entering into a negotiation are either too lazy to spend the time to preplan, or they simply don't know how.

When you can anticipate questions from the other side in a negotiation you can tailor favorable responses to them. Preplanning gives you the ability to offer a timely well-conceived answer that induces a sense of satisfaction in the person asking the question. By preplanning the answer to a question that likely will be asked, you can deliver a thoughtful response with spontaneity, as if you had just thought of it. For instance, you could say, "This might be a workable plan." Or "What about if we try this?" The fact that your intuitive way of thinking is right in line with theirs, along with your impromptu insight, helps to develop a feeling of relaxed mutual trust.

Preplanning also includes providing data from magazines or newspaper articles to support and reinforce your positions. Statistics too, especially if they are from seemingly reliable sources, can also be effective in convincing the other side.

Be a Good Listener

When you listen carefully to the arguments and objections of the other side, you can determine what they really want. Frequently, people in negotiation try to get results indirectly. If you can, somehow, bring forth what the other side really wants, the negotiations will have more of a successful outcome. Often, you'll find that disagreements simply stem from lack of communication: two adversaries not communicating what they think they are communicating. In negotiations, most often it's better to be a good listener than a talker.

Negotiation Tactics

To set the stage for successful negotiations, consider the following tactics:

- *Avoid making the initial offer (he or she who speaks first, loses).* Allow the opposing party to initiate negotiations. Why? Because it's possible that their initial offering will be below your proposed offer. For example, suppose that after studying all the data about a potential acquisition, you determine that you're willing to offer \$120,000 to start negotiations. In fact, you're willing to pay up to \$135,000 for the property. But perhaps the seller is uninformed of its true market value and is willing to sell the property for no less than \$100,000. And of course, you don't know this information. Meanwhile, because you're a novice negotiator, you unfortunately begin the negotiations by offering \$120,000. You probably could have saved \$10,000 to \$20,000 just by keeping your mouth shut and letting the seller start negotiations. The seller in this scenario could feasibly open negotiations at \$110,000 and you could negotiate the price down to \$100,000. But if you have already opened the bidding at \$120,000, you have no where to go. The seller will either accept your bid or counter at a higher price.
- *Don't be an unfriendly bad guy.* Instead, you want to be a nice person with a friendly personality. You need to make others feel comfortable in talking and dealing with you. Again, find common ground for chitchat. Find out about the other party's interests. The greater interest you show in them, the more you encourage a warm, nonhostile feeling.
- *Don't accept any offer quickly.* Take your time in making a crucial decision. Even if it's your decision to make, hold back, and put the decision on someone else, even if that "someone" does not exist. Tell them, for instance, that you have to discuss the situation with your superiors or your spouse (even if you're the only decision maker). This way you have time to carefully consider important factors.

Furthermore, a skilled negotiator can use pressure to make the other side arrive at a decision quickly, and that decision might not have been made otherwise had the adversary spent sufficient time contemplating crucial factors. It's always best to take your time, especially when there's a lot at stake.

Overly quick negotiations leave one side unsatisfied. The reason is that each party must feel he or she achieved a number of sought-after concessions from his or her adversary; otherwise, his or her ego is not satisfied, and he or she feels as though he or she didn't do a good job.

Here's an example: I want to sell my almost-new Troy-Bilt riding lawnmower with a 42-inch cut. It's in great shape with only 11 hours on the engine at a price of $1,200. You call me up and say, "I'll give you $900." And I quickly respond with, "You have a deal." You just purchased a $1,200 lawnmower for $900. But are you happy? No! Because I accepted your offer too quickly, which makes you feel that you could have bought it for less and saved $200 or $300. This is an example of accepting an offer too quickly, because the buyer is unhappy. If he or she has the opportunity, he or she may try to find a way to get out of the deal.

In this example, the buyer isn't happy because there wasn't enough time spent going through the bargaining process. The buyer has to be convinced that he or she bought it for the cheapest price and got the most out of the negotiation. The whole process, the haggling, the arguing back and forth, takes time to accomplish.

Another reason not to accept a quick deal is that one party will surely omit something. And the oversight will become apparent only after the deal is closed, when it's too late to correct the problem.

- *Don't believe in the "bogus buyer."* The bogus buyer is someone artificial inserted into negotiations for the purpose of stimulating action. It's a nonexistent buyer invented by the seller. The bogus buyer enters the negotiations in ways like this: During negotiations the seller says to you, "Look, if you don't want the deal, I have someone else who will pay full list price." Or "I've got better offers from two other buyers." Don't give those counterfeit statements any credibility. If the claims were valid, the sellers wouldn't be dealing with you; instead, they'd be working on the other, better deal.
- *Don't ever discuss your weaknesses.* This means you and everyone on your team should never talk about your weaknesses in front of

anyone at any time. Many transactions have failed because non-negotiators opened their big mouths.

- *Don't enter into a bidding war.* The added competition makes it difficult to purchase a bargain-priced property. It's always better to buy from a motivated seller who will make concessions than it is to compete with other buyers who are trying to outbid each other. Remember the old saying, "There are always more fish in the sea." And likewise, there will always be more desirable properties on the market—you only need to spend the necessary time to find them.

Beware of Other Negotiation Ploys

Consider the following situation. A man named McGuire is prepared to sell a building for $15 million. An interested buyer comes along and offers him $15 million. But McGuire says, "You've got to do better than that."

So the other side replies, "Well, how about $16 million."

Again, McGuire replies, "You've got to do better than that."

Now McGuire has already made a million dollars, and he was willing to accept $15 million, but just by saying "You've got to do better than that," he makes the other side feel that they have to increase their offer so they won't lose the transaction.

So watch out for this ploy because it works!

As a counterploy, you could easily say, "Why do I have to do better than that? I think it's a fair price."

The negotiation principles and tactics I described can be effective, and they can sway the other side to your way of thinking, but they won't work for everyone. It's crucial that you adopt your own style of negotiating. To simply copy someone else is a mistake: The opposition can sense your insincerity, which is a quick turnoff that will lead them to distrust you.

Structuring the Purchase Contract

The following material addresses the more important issues buyers and sellers should consider when structuring the purchase contract.

The most important thing to remember about this phase is that your overall purpose is to make everything in the contract perfectly clear.

Moreover, you want to make it easy for a disinterested third party to interpret your meaning so that there will be nothing left to decide at a later date.

Names of the Parties

It's very important that your written purchase contract include *all* individuals involved in the transaction. You need to be especially sure that all owners (sellers) are named and that each of them is available to sign your written offer once an agreement is reached. You have to be cautious in dealing with a seller whose spouse or co-owners are not actively involved in negotiations because if they don't agree to sign your offer, there is no deal.

Putting the decision on someone else is one of the oldest negotiating ploys around; and it often works. Here's the scenario: The seller tells you that his or her spouse (or partners) will agree to whatever the seller says. But once everything is written down and you think you've made a deal, the seller surprises you and says, "You're not going to believe this, but my wife refuses to sign. She thinks I'm giving the house away, and she wants another $30,000. But I've told her that I can't back out and change the deal now. But she is adamant about the price. So I'll work a deal with you, which should pacify her. If we split the difference and increase your offer another $15,000, I'll go back and try to convince her to accept it." And then the seller closes his routine with, "I'm really sorry about this unforeseen event, but my wife, at times, can be difficult to reason with."

You can avoid this bad situation by not negotiating with someone who lacks the legal authority to negotiate and carry out the written agreement. In other words, make sure you're, in fact, dealing with all the owners when you are negotiating and writing the purchase contract.

Price and Financing

When preparing your offer, be specific about the purchase price and all the details concerning the financing. Spell out the purchase price, specify the down payment, and list the balance due, when it's payable, how it will be paid, and at what rate of interest. Again, be precise and don't leave anything open to interpretation or speculation.

The same holds true if you're planning to arrange new financing, or if you're assuming the seller's mortgage. Omission of the terms of financing leaves too many unanswered questions. If you intend to arrange new financing, spell out the maximum limits, such as 7.5 percent interest and 20 percent down for 30 years. Then, if you cannot get a mortgage within those limits, you're not obligated to complete the purchase.

Site Description

The subject property needs to be properly identified by street address and legal description. As a precaution, refer to your survey or plat map, and walk the boundaries of the property. Try to estimate the size of the property and determine whether it resembles the property you're actually receiving. While walking the perimeter, note the boundaries and any encroachments. You want to visually verify where surveyed boundaries actually lie.

Personal Property

Real property is the land and all the improvements attached to it. And, generally speaking, *personal property* refers to all items not permanently attached to the buildings (improvements) or land. Since your purchase agreement does not include the personal property that may be part of your purchase contract with the sellers, you need to list these items in your written purchase agreement.

For instance, if you're purchasing an apartment building and the sellers have provided the tenants with miniblinds, ranges, and built-in microwaves, spell out these items in an addendum and attach it to your purchase agreement.

Listing personal property serves another purpose too: It identifies what property belongs to the landlord and what belongs to the tenants. Then later, after you buy the property, you can settle any disputes with the tenants over who owns what with an accurate list of personal property that the sellers transferred to you.

Remember that the art of negotiation is more than just haggling over price and terms. It involves mastering preparation, understanding human nature, learning how to uncover and exploit weaknesses, and many other intricacies. When you apply the bargaining principles and tactics brought forth in this chapter, you will definitely be on your way to making better deals in real estate.

9

Fixing Up the Fixer-Upper

Key Points

- *What to look for in a fixer-upper*
- *Improvements that pay*
- *No-no improvements*
- *Necessary repairs and improvements*
- *Hiring a contractor and controlling costs*

A so-called fixer-upper isn't necessarily a run-down property that needs fixing up. To the contrary, a fixer-upper can also be a property that's in good condition physically, yet needs a little fine-tuning to make it more desirable. These relatively minor changes to the property may include such things as a thorough cleaning, enhanced curb appeal, more appealing kitchen and bathrooms, added usable space, or added pizzazz with better color schemes and fixtures.

A good example is a home we purchased in 1986 on the southwest side of Las Vegas, Nevada. It was a rather plain-looking custom-built home with

2,200 square feet of living area. It had a tile roof and a three-car garage and was situated on a half-acre of horse-zoned real estate. The home was in great shape; it just needed a few alterations to make it more appealing. For example, when entering the home through the front door, you dropped down into a sunken living room that had dreadful carpet on the floors. And instead of wood baseboards, along the room's perimeter it had carpeting that extended up the wall eight inches. We decided right away that the living room carpet, including the horrible carpeted baseboards, had to go.

The remainder of the house, except for the kitchen, which had solid oak cabinets throughout, was very plain and lacked any character whatsoever. All of the walls were painted in off-white, and there was no wood or wallpaper anywhere.

The first alteration we made was to pull up that living room carpet and the pad underneath it. Then we installed beautiful tongue-and-groove golden-oak floors over the concrete slab. Wow! The wood looked so magnificent, and it made a great first impression when you entered the room through the front door. Next, we attached eight-inch strips of solid oak, laid at a 45-degree angle, on two walls in the living room near the entry. Then we stained the oak to match the tone of the golden-oak flooring. For the finishing touch, we encased both archways in the living room and adjacent dining room with oak trim molding, which we stained with two coats satin gloss polyurethane.

My wife and I did the whole project ourselves. We not only found the entire renovation to be a true pleasure to work on and to see materialize but the whole project cost less than $1,000 in materials. Our neighbors were impressed with the change that was made, and everybody that saw it loved all the new woodwork. But the final satisfaction came when we lease/purchase-optioned the house for a handsome $20,000 profit four months after we bought it. I truly believe that we would not have made as much profit nor received such a great positive response had we not added that finished woodwork to that once very plain house.

What to Look for in a Fixer-Upper

Keep an eye out for ways to improve a particular property without expending too much money and effort. Anyone can overspend and turn a virtual dump into a desirable mansion. But there's no value in doing that. A wise investor is someone who can see through the imperfections and has the vision and the courage to assemble the financial resources to make the right practical improvements that will do the most to substantially increase the value of the property. A fixer-upper buyer creates value by adding *sweat equity* (adding value by doing the renovations himself or herself). If you believe you fit that mold, here's what you can expect to achieve after converting your unpolished gem into an exquisite diamond:

- You will own a home or an income property for a lot less than you could otherwise have afforded to buy.
- The property will be redesigned and decorated the way you like it, instead of its reflecting someone else's concept of style and taste.
- And you will have substantially increased the property's value in excess of the cost to make the renovations.

How to Develop a Market-Sensitive Fix-Up Strategy

You might ask, "What are the rules for creating value when I buy a property?" There are none! Features that one person likes, another hates. What's popular in a south Florida high-rise condominium may be out of place in an upper-east-side Manhattan flat. Likewise, amenities admired in the desert southwest would be inappropriate in the New England states. And certain home features that appeal to you may not suit the lifestyles and tastes of most people. Money spent to redo a kitchen in Chicago might return $2 for each $1 invested, while in Houston, returns for a similar renovation might be a losing proposition with a meager 50 cents for every $1 invested.

With so many variables to think about, how does one satisfy the tastes and lifestyles of potential prospects who will look over your property? Put your own personal tastes aside and follow the guidelines of successful home builders. They carefully research the market to determine precisely what home buyers want.

You can start by asking local Realtors what home buyers are looking for in a home. Also you can visit new home developments, taking special note of their decorating themes, floor plans, floor covering materials, and countertops. While you're touring the models, make inquiries about what amenities and features are in most demand and which ones are rarely chosen.

Visit open houses too, seeking ways other property owners have improved and decorated their homes. Also check out what some of the major home-improvement outlets in your area have, such as Lowe's and Home Depot, and talk to the associates who work there. And while you're there, browse through some of the how-to books on home improvement.

Improvements That Pay

Granted, there are no absolute rules etched in stone on how to create value in real estate: There are, however, some practical guidelines that can be applied to deciding whether a property is worth fixing up and which improvements are sensible and worthwhile investments.

While you're out searching for worthwhile properties, you have to look at them in a certain way. You must disregard your first impressions and enthusiasm. Rather, determine what's wrong with the properties—why you find them unappealing—then try to arrive at practical solutions. Looking at them this way will help you narrow down your list of possible investments. Ask yourself, which of these could I renovate and decorate in such a way and at such a cost that it would be more appealing to prospective buyers than it is now and therefore likely to turn a profit for me?

For example, let's say you find a house that at first seems very nice, but it's a five-bedroom two-bath dwelling with only 1,800 square feet of living area. The problem is that the bedrooms are too small, which is why it is not appealing as much as it could to most potential tenants and buyers. In deciding whether to buy the house or not, you realize you would need to economically knock out a few walls and convert this dwelling with five small bedrooms into a more practical home with three large bedrooms. So the question for you becomes, would the converted house's value and appeal be worth the capital investment and effort you have to make? To answer that question, consider the following two-for-one guideline.

The Two-for-One Guideline

This is a basic guideline that says that every $1 invested in renovation should yield at least $2 in increased property value. So, for example, house renovations that cost $10,000 should realize at least $20,000 in market value gain.

Often you'll find neglected properties that have been given little care and attention. You'll notice overgrown bushes, a weed-infested lawn with trash strewn about, pealing exterior paint, and a few broken windows. But if the house is structurally sound and everything else checks out (such as the roof, electrical wiring, and plumbing), all this mess and disrepair presents a great opportunity for the fixer-upper investor with foresight.

To determine whether this is indeed a good buy, all you have to do is estimate what it will cost to get the landscaping in shape and to clean up and renovate the property. You then double that cost figure (the two-for-one guideline) to see how much the improvements would add to the value of the property. Then you add that value-added figure to your cost to purchase the property. Then ask yourself, will I be able to sell the renovated property at a price that will result in a worthwhile profit for me?

Put another way, after renovations are complete, will the property be worth at least what you paid for it, plus double the cost of renovating it? If the answer is yes, then it's probably a wise investment and a prime candidate for profitable renovation.

The Improvements Most Likely to Increase Property Value

The following practical improvements will usually make a property more appealing to prospective buyers and thereby increase its value:

- Cleaning the property thoroughly inside and out
- Improving the curb appeal
- Paying attention to the most important rooms: the kitchen and the bathrooms (not the bedrooms)
- Creating additional usable space
- Adding pizzazz by updating the color schemes and fixtures
- Reducing noise

Cleaning the Property Thoroughly Inside and Out

Regardless of whether you intend to sell or rent the property, it's crucial that it be thoroughly cleaned before you show it to any prospects. The reason is that a spotlessly clean house or unit will not only rent or sell more quickly, but it will also most certainly attract a more reliable tenant who can pay a higher rent or a buyer who can afford a higher-priced property.

In the case of rental properties, many lackadaisical property owners take the position, "Why should I go to the trouble of giving a spotlessly clean unit to tenants because they'll only leave it dirty when they move out anyway?" Such an attitude only begets poor results. Quality buyers and renters are repulsed by filth, and they will choose to live elsewhere. The kind of people who accept rental units with grime-encrusted stoves, soiled carpets, and filthy windows are the same kind who won't care for your property.

Cleanliness is especially important in the kitchen and bathrooms. Make an extra effort to remove dirt and stains on countertops, bathtubs, sinks, toilet bowls, and mirrors.

When you demonstrate cleanliness in your available units, you'll achieve four positive things: (1) You'll attract a better grade of tenant; (2) you'll earn a higher rental rate; (3) you'll display to your tenants the level of cleanliness you expect; and (4) you'll be able to get a better price when you do sell because investors will pay more for properties with better tenants simply because better clientele will mean to them, as it does to you, less trouble, lower risk, and more reliable rental income.

Improving the Curb Appeal

The purpose here is to attract passersby. You want them to pull over in their car, get out, and look at what you have to offer. At the very least, you want them to stop long enough and with sufficient interest to take down your address and phone number and come back later. You can attract this type of serious interest by improving the curb appeal of the property. Most home buyers and renters decide whether or not to look inside a house based on its *curb appeal*—that is, the view they see when they drive by or arrive for a showing. You improve the property's curb appeal by dressing up its exterior appearance.

Enhancing the landscaping of the exterior is one method. Instead of arbitrarily putting in three or four nondescript bushes around a building's foundation, carefully conceive a planting scheme that will look appropriate in the area and that can be easily maintained. One way to project an image of easy maintenance is to choose plants that are not fast growers and are therefore not apt to become overgrown too quickly.

Consider hiring a landscape designer. Many are not expensive, and the good ones know how to boost curb appeal. You and/or your designer can create a landscape that gives the impression of desirability and easy maintenance. Landscape designers will be able to suggest plantings that augment the topography of the site as well as the size and shape of the site. They can also emphasize or deemphasize the built structures on the site to attract attention to those features on the site that you want to be noticed.

The whole concept of curb appeal is visual. It is perceived value. It doesn't have to be expensive, but it has to be *perceived* as valuable. Creating curb appeal can be accomplished by the choice of colors, by the types of plantings, and so on, so that prospects say, "This looks like a wonderful place to live." They "perceive" value through your well-conceived plantings or your tasteful use of color on the dwelling, and your lovely landscaped site. These images all blend together to portray your project as a desirable place to live.

What other features can make a property appear desirable? Besides the enhanced landscaping, a curb-appeal feature could also be the brass hardware on the door or the type of wood that the door is made from. Or it could be the window treatments. Or it could be a piece of Japanese sculpture you put in the garden area to add visual interest. It could be a curved walkway bordered by majestic Italian cypress trees that lead up to the garden.

All of these things and many others can make a property extremely desirable. These enhancements are not necessarily expensive. Rather, the value from them is added by the intelligent way of blending certain things together to create a perception of value.

Paying Attention to the Most Important Rooms: Kitchens and Bathrooms

When it comes to the interior of the house, concentrate on improvements to the kitchen and bathrooms, not the other rooms. If you hold back on making improvements in the kitchen and bath areas, you'll have a problem attracting the luxury customer. What appeals to most house-hunting people more than anything else are the features and spaciousness of the kitchen and bathrooms. Not the bedrooms. The first thing the woman of the house looks for is practical and appealing kitchen and bathrooms.

There's an old saying among seasoned Realtors that goes like this: When a husband and wife are looking to buy a house, the first thing the wife considers is the kitchen and bathrooms; the husband's first concern is whether or not the payments on the house are affordable.

When you're thinking about the renovation of the kitchen, instead of common laminates, consider installing countertops of granite or solid surface materials such as Avonite or Corian. These materials cost more, but they are eye-catching and will help create the perceived value you're trying to achieve. And don't be a penny-pincher when it comes to the kitchen. Install great-looking cabinets, lots of storage space, a large pantry, and a center island work place. Also in the kitchen go the extra mile and use first-line appliances. If, for example, you're installing a refrigerator, be sure it's a Subzero model with a top-of-the-line ice maker. Make sure the kitchen is well designed for convenience with lots of space. When you have a lot of great features and amenities, the house will be more appealing. You want your prospect to think, "This kitchen is gorgeous, and it's got everything I need."

When renovating bathrooms, think spaciousness. Upscale buyers or tenants are looking for more space, so give them as much as circumstances allow. Put extra money in vanities, countertops, and light fixtures. Instead of just a plain bathtub, if possible, make it a whirlpool tub, and in the stall shower have the added feature of a steam unit. Lots of storage space and soothing color combinations, such as a nice blend of earth tones, are also appealing.

Other attractive features are spacious closets with built-ins such as adjustable shelving and shoe racks.

You always need to ask yourself, "Where can I effectively spend my renovation dollars to make the greatest visual impact?" The answer most often is usually in the kitchen and the bathrooms.

Creating Additional Usable Space

The objective here is to figure out how to economically create additional usable space, which in turn increases the market value of the property.

Forget about converting the garage into living area because it's already a useful place to store your cars, or whatever. Homeowners who convert their garages into living areas are making a terrible mistake because the lack of a garage seriously inhibits the marketability of the house. Potential home buyers or renters prefer having a garage because it provides a great storage place for vehicles and other miscellaneous items.

But perhaps a property you are considering has an attic or basement that can be converted into additional living area. Or could you enclose a patio or porch? Perhaps add a second story, or construct a guest apartment? What about combining small rooms to make larger rooms (such as converting five small bedrooms into three large bedrooms as discussed earlier)?

Adding Pizzazz by Updating the Color Schemes and Fixtures

Frequently, when it comes to a home's appealing features and tastefully appointed home décor, it's the simple little things that count the most. That big plain-looking ranch home that we owned in Las Vegas that I mentioned earlier is a good example. The exterior walls were stucco and painted beige with no window treatments whatsoever. Looking at it from the street, I realized that the front elevation needed some decorating, but at first I was unsure of what to do about it. So I drove around the neighborhood viewing other homes. Finally, I realized what was missing: shutters around the front windows. I went to Home Depot and purchased three sets of wood shutters. When I got home, I painted them dark brown for contrast with the beige stucco, and then I installed them next to the windows along the front elevation. Against the beige walls, the shutters looked great, and they really added pizzazz to what was once a very drab looking home.

You can also enhance the appeal of the dwelling's interior. You can redo the walls and trim with modern color schemes, or put up decorative wallpapers and borders, or decorate with other special touches. Adding polished granite or ceramic tile to an entry or kitchen floor can really dress up what would otherwise be a plain-looking home. The addition of special moldings too, such as a stained chair rail in the dining room or kitchen or crown molding in the living room or master bedroom, can create a special ambience. And you can replace older, drab-looking light fixtures with modern decorative ones. Remember to keep it simple but tasteful. Too much of anything can become garish. By adding just the right amount of flair and creative design touches, you can make what was once commonplace very interesting and desirable.

Reducing Noise

Excessive noise costs property owners a lot of money because it's a big nuisance. In multiunit buildings especially, too much noise will cause too much turnover among your tenants. When you're considering the purchase of an attached home (like a condo or co-op) or a multiunit building, be sure to check the soundproofing between the units. If you put your ear up to the wall and you can hear a television, a toilet flush, or people talking in the adjacent unit, be wary. Unless you have a way of overcoming this noise problem, you'll be faced with a never-ending stream of tenant complaints and a high level of tenant turnover.

Consider noise also when looking at detached buildings and properties. If you discover a noise problem, then before you make your initial offer to buy a particular property, consider the feasibility of reducing the noise. Can you add more wall insulation, soundproof some or all of the windows, build a block wall, construct an earth berm, or plant trees or shrubs?

Most homeowners and tenants will pay a premium for peace and quiet, and many won't tolerate too much noise.

No-No Improvements

Most experienced realty investors have developed a list of repairs or improvements to avoid. Acclaimed syndicated columnist Robert Bruss says, "Smart fixer-upper home buyers and investors look for properties with the right things wrong." To Bruss, the "right things wrong" include cosmetic improvements such as painting, landscaping, carpets, and light fixtures. On his list of no-nos are roofs, foundations, wiring, and plumbing.

Although Bruss offers sound advice, there are certain exceptions. In 1976 I knew of a foreclosed house in Pasadena, California, that sat on the market for over a year because of foundation problems. The house itself was structurally sound, but the foundation was crumbling, and because of that, no lenders would underwrite a mortgage on it. The property was situated in the midst of $100,000 homes, but it was being offered for $15,000 cash. Still there were no takers. Eventually a fellow who happened to be a professional house mover came along and bought it. He then jacked up the house 12 feet, knocked out the old stone foundation, poured a new foundation, and sat the house back down on its new foundation. He then sold the completed project for a $42,000 profit. With a new concrete foundation, he had no trouble selling the property because mortgage lenders found the new foundation an acceptable risk. Not too bad for three months' work.

Converting the Garage to a Rental

Foremost among the no-no improvements is the garage conversion. Many investors are inclined to alter the garage into more living space or convert it into a living area. But, as briefly mentioned earlier, in doing so, you most often seriously inhibit the salability of the property. Why? Because you no longer have a garage, which is a great place to store and protect many of your valued personal items, such as vehicles, lawn and garden equipment, and tools. It's also a great place to have a useful workbench. If you need more living area, build something new attached to the existing living area of the house instead of eliminating functional garage space that is already useful. Most house-hunting prospects require a garage as a valuable storage facility.

Necessary Repairs and Improvements

Many property owners skimp on regular upkeep and defer maintenance projects on their properties, which can have disastrous results. If the property consists of rental units, inevitably, as the property gradually deteriorates from lack of proper care, quality tenants find somewhere else to live. The loss of good clientele means lower rent levels, which in turn results in reduced cash flow for the owner. As the property gradually loses its appeal, it deteriorates further until the rundown property has to be sold at a reduced price. This negative scenario is very typical of property owners who have the misconception that they can save money by deferring maintenance.

In order to optimize your income and keep your properties at their highest market value, it's necessary to always maintain them in A-1 condition. This means at all times—not just the day you're showing them to prospective buyers or tenants. All systems have to be in working order at all times, and the property must be thoroughly clean and showing no signs of wear or abuse. This is important because any prospects viewing the property, either as potential buyers or rent-paying tenants, will discount from the value of the property anything dirty or in disrepair. Or even worse, they may become repulsed and just stop in their tracks, turn around, and go looking for something else more appealing.

The following items deserve special attention in the regular maintenance of any property.

Air-Conditioning and Heating

Among the biggest turnoffs for prospective buyers or tenants are dirty, grime-laden heat ducts and registers. They're usually the result of a dirty intake filter. If the prospects find a dirty filter, they could rightfully presume that it was never changed regularly, and they would thus suspect that the system itself could be damaged. Be sure to always change intake furnace and air-conditioning filters monthly (and instruct your tenants to do the same), and make sure that the registers and ducts are clean and the systems are operating effectively.

Electrical

Make sure all light bulbs are working properly. If you have any fluorescent bulbs, replace the weaker flickering ones and the ones that are slow to light. It's also a good idea to check the building's fuse or breaker box to make sure it's in good working order. Find out the amperage coming into the property. Nowadays a typical three-bedroom home requires at least 100 amperes. Anything less will require an upgrade. Inspect electrical outlets and their covers. Charred or broken ones need to be replaced. An electrical outlet should never have many adapters or extension cords plugged into it. Such a condition is a fire hazard, and it is evidence that there are insufficient electrical outlets.

Plumbing

Inspect all faucets for leaks and drips. Dripping faucets need the washers replaced. Sink and bathtub drains need to empty quickly; if they don't, the traps need cleaning out. Inspect toilet tanks to be sure that the float automatically shuts off the fill valve. Toilet seats that are stained or in disrepair must be replaced. Inspect for leaks around the bathtub perimeter and shower stalls. Apply caulking to seal leaks or repair cracks. Water stains are tantamount to waving a red flag in the face of prospects warning them of a plumbing problem. In the northern latitudes, water pipes exposed to the weather need insulation to keep them from bursting in cold weather.

Appliances

For rental properties, when you provide appliances, they must be spotlessly clean and fully operational. Be sure to keep the appliance owner's manuals in a handy place where the tenants have access to them.

Walls and Ceilings

Avoid vivid dark colors. For the interior of your dwellings, use light earth tones and neutral colors that will blend with people's furnishings. Repair cracks in plaster and wallboard with spackling, sand the areas smooth, and then repaint. Maintain a bright, cheerful ambience throughout the home or rental unit.

Windows and Screens

Repair any windows that are painted shut. Windows that do not open and close easily are a real turnoff to potential occupants. Replace all cracked glass, and repair all pulleys and damaged frames, including damaged weather stripping. Replace all broken or torn screens.

Doors and Locks

Every door should open and close properly, without squeaking or being overly tight. Squeaky hinges need to be lubricated. Doors that are too snug can be planed down. Replace any damaged screening on screen doors. And for security purposes it would be wise to replace worn-out or broken locks.

Landscaping

Properly maintained landscaping makes your property more desirable (remember curb appeal). If your prospects form a negative first impression of your property, they may forget about getting out of their vehicle and instead, just go on to the next property. To avoid that, pay attention to the landscaping of your property. Rake up any fallen leaves and keep the lawn mowed. And don't forget to trim the shrubs and trees and remove any dead or unattractive bushes.

Storage Areas

All storage areas, including the garage and basement, have to be tidied up. Items you don't need or want anymore can be given away or liquidated at a garage sale (think of the extra space along with the money you earn). You will have to clean up these areas anyway before the buyers or tenants take possession. So try to get this work accomplished before you show the property to anyone, because cleaned-out storage areas will give the dwelling a more spacious look.

Hiring a Contractor and Controlling Costs

Whether you hire a contractor to do the repairs and renovations depends on whether you have adequate fix-up funds and how much work you're capable of doing yourself and thereby earning "sweat equity." If you have plenty of cash and are in a big hurry to invest in more real estate, then hire contractors to accomplish the renovations work. But it will be more profitable for you to do the work yourself. Personally, I enjoy doing much of the work. I hire contractors only for the work that I'm not capable of doing, such as laying carpet and working on some parts of the electrical systems. Over the years when I have had to hire contractors, I have watched carefully and asked them plenty of questions—then afterward I was often capable of doing the job myself.

When you hire a contractor, follow these guidelines:

- Get references on the quality of their work. Good contractors build their business on their reputations, and their satisfied customers will be your best references.

- Make inquiries with at least two contractors, and get written bids for the work you expect to be completed.
- Have the contractor provide you with three references, and then check them out. Phone each reference and ask if there were any problems with the job. If there were problems, did the contractor correct them? Check also on whether the contractor assessed any extra charges on top of the original estimates, and ask if the contractor completed the job on time.
- Have a preliminary plan drawn up that you can show to the contractor. A floor plan drawn to scale with certain specifications would give the contractor something substantial to work with.

To save money buy materials in the off season when the stores are having sales to stimulate business and when contractors are not very busy, such as the period between Thanksgiving and the end of February. A down-time period is a great time to find contractors since they are not as busy as they usually are.

When it comes to handling construction and renovations, you need to learn as much as you can about every aspect of the real estate business. The more knowledge you have about prices, costs, options, materials, real estate services, and so on, the more opportunities you will have to reduce costs and increase profits.

Chapter Summary

When it comes to fixer-uppers, keep in mind that that almost anyone can do the simple things—such as cleaning and painting the property. It's the more difficult things that create the greatest opportunities for making profits. You need to look for those special properties that have problems that are difficult but not impossible to overcome. Many investors lack imagination, and the minute they walk through the door and see things they don't like, they say, "No way. Let's look for something else to buy." If you are knowledgeable about how to make and finance needed renovations, you will come out way ahead of these other investors.

Problems that can usually be overcome include such things as the design and use of the living-area space (such as converting a small five-bedroom house into a more desirable home with three spacious bedrooms) and poorly designed or equipped kitchens and bathrooms.

To develop a sound strategy for investing in fixer-uppers, make inquiries with successful home builders and developers in your area to see what buyers are looking for. In this way you can make market-sensitive improvements. You should always be thinking when you're looking at a potential purchase, "What can I do to overcome the defects and improve the appeal of this property?" And then, ask yourself, "Will those improvements add enough value to make the investment worthwhile (keeping in mind the two-for-one guideline)?"

10

Managing Your Real Estate

Guidelines for Hassle-Free Operations and Optimizing Profits

Key Points

- *Making people want to be in your building*
- *Managing multiunit buildings*
- *Setting up furnished versus unfurnished apartments*
- *Attracting good tenants*
- *Showing and renting available units*
- *Drafting the best rental agreement*
- *Managing the move-in*
- *Managing the rent collection*
- *Eviction procedures for nonpayment of rent*
- *Budgeting*
- *Keeping records*
- *Managing repairs*
- *The four "nevers" of successful property management*

Properly managed, a well-selected piece of income property is the closest thing you will ever find to a thriving, self-generating money machine. When you've got the right resident manager on site, and you have made the time and effort to carefully choose the tenants that live there, and you have learned how to do certain procedures the right way, then you will be able to handle most of your work over the phone with occasional monthly visits to the property. Collecting rent, screening prospective tenants, showing vacancies, overseeing maintenance and repairs, and budgeting do not require hard work. However, they do require you to take the time to learn to be proficient. And underlying the proficiency you need to acquire is the understanding that successful real estate management is about managing people. This includes overseeing a resident manager if you own a multiunit building or directly handling the tenants of the homes you rent. Whatever the case, you have to know how to manage people so that they can efficiently do most of the work for you.

I like to refer to this approach as "McLean's guide to optimizing profits and hassle-free property management." That's because in this chapter you're going to learn how to avoid the normal nuisances—the ones the inexperienced and naïve rental owners face every day—and learn how to overcome the hassles and do things efficiently, the right way.

Being a successful landlord is no accident. It can be a wonderful learning experience as you reap all the rewards of operating a profitable, moneymaking income property. On the other hand, poorly managed real estate can drain your resources and be a burdensome daily chore. Bad management is not only a burden on your finances; it's also an active drain on your time and energy. It can turn a potentially good investment into an unwanted nightmare. However, when you hire the right people and do things the proper way, you not only will make the most from your investment but you will also be able to just about put your realty holdings on automatic pilot and go away on a long vacation.

Making People Want to Be in Your Property

Far too many landlords are inferior, miserly property managers who view their tenants as necessary evils. They look upon them not as valued customers but instead as headaches that are always complaining and never seem to be satisfied. All of this presents a great opportunity for the smart investor who sees property management as a customer-service business and treats his or her tenants as valued customers. How can you make people want to be in your building? You can do it in the following ways:

- Keep the property extraordinarily clean, inside and out. Tenants will pay more for an immaculately maintained building than they will for one that looks just so-so.
- Provide extra household features for tenants instead of merely supplying them with living quarters. Invest your money in special features that can be readily seen, such as a center island in the kitchen, granite countertops, or top-of-the-line cabinets. In the bathroom, install a special lighted mirror for putting on makeup.
- Provide special customer service. For example, the resident manager or superintendent could perform a special service such as receiving and mailing packages.
- Provide fast service for needed repairs. Hire a resident manager or an all-around maintenance worker who can do odd jobs so that someone who has a pleasant customer-service attitude will be readily available almost all the time.

When you or your resident manager is oriented toward customers and delights tenants with a pleasant and courteous attitude and is willing to serve customer needs, you will gain a great advantage over the competition.

Managing Multiunit Buildings

Regardless of whether you own one rental home, a fourplex, or a large 20-unit apartment building, most of the guidelines presented in this chapter still apply. However, if you own more than one rental unit on a particular site—such as a duplex or a fourplex, instead of a single-family home—you need to have someone responsible for certain duties living on the premises. These duties include being responsible for showing vacancies, collecting rents, and generally overseeing the property.

In the 20-unit building, the responsible person is the resident manager whom the owner has delegated to assume certain responsibilities. But even with the smaller rental properties, the owner still needs to have someone on site who is responsible for certain duties. This can include showing vacancies, maintaining the grounds, and opening a door for a locked-out tenant in the middle of the night. This way, by the owner's delegating certain responsibilities to an on-site tenant, he or she alleviates many of the menial duties that can be a landlord's nuisance.

The responsible person is your liaison between you and the tenants. So instead of your having to drive all the way over to the property to show a vacant unit, you can have your manager do it. Or if a tenant has lost his or her key at two o'clock in the morning, the manager instead of you can let him or her in. Your manager can also be instructed on showing vacancies and having prospective tenants fill out the application to rent, which when completed can then be forwarded to you. (For sample forms, including the *application to rent* and *rental agreement*, see the appendix at the end of the book.)

Choosing the Resident Manager

The ideal situation is a husband and wife team. Typically the wife will have the full-time responsibility as the resident manager since she will more likely be at home most of the time and will not have a full-time job elsewhere. The husband will usually have a full-time job but can still do some maintenance such as mowing the lawn and function as a part-time maintenance and repair worker.

The following are the chief characteristics you should look for in a resident manager:

- Has the ability to accept responsibility and adhere to the owner's guidelines
- Has a spouse who has a full-time job but at the same time is willing and able to be a part-time maintenance and repair worker on the property
- Has a pleasant personality and is willing to give the tenants the ultimate in customer service.
- Has a willingness to stay at home and assist in the overall operation of the property

Resident Manager's Duties

Above all, it's the manager's responsibility to adhere to the guidelines the owner of the property sets forth. Depending on the size of the property being managed, this can include rent collection, record keeping, showing vacancies, and maintaining the common grounds. When the resident manager or the spouse is capable of making repairs and taking care of the landscaping, then you eliminate the need to hire a professional repair person or a lawn maintenance service.

It's very important that the resident manager agree to stay at home and be on the job to show vacancies and keep order around the building. Someone who is active outside the home—a person with a full- or part-time job or with numerous social commitments—is not a good prospect. A parent who prefers to stay at home with children typically is better suited as an on-site manager.

What you pay a typical husband and wife management team depends on the size of the building being managed and the duties you assign them. Free rent of a two-bedroom apartment is common in a 20-unit apartment building. On a smaller building, such as a 4- or 6-unit building, a 25 percent reduction in rent would be common. Buildings larger than 20 units usually involve free rent plus a cash salary. For competitive salaries in your area, look in the local newspaper in the classified section under the column "Couples Wanted."

Landlord Tale

When I managed 363 rental units in 1976, I earned a salary of $1,200 per month, which included a complimentary one-bedroom apartment. But I worked at least 60 hours a week, and I supervised a staff of 10 employees, which included 2 leasing agents, 1 repair person, 2 painters, 1 housekeeper, 2 carpet cleaners, 1 security guard, and 1 activity director. With this staff and if the unit didn't need excessive repairs, we were capable of moving out the departing tenant in the morning, completely renovating the apartment—cleaning, painting, and shampooing the carpets—and then moving in the new tenant by 4:30 in the afternoon of the same day. Overall, we were able to keep vacancies at about 1 percent during the two years I was there. Not bad, considering the national average vacancy rate was then and still is about 5 percent annually.

Supervising the Resident Manager

The duties of the resident manager must be fully explained at the outset of the owner-employee relationship. Be sure the manager knows exactly what is expected of him or her. Remember, the more responsibility you can delegate to the manager, the more time you will have for other matters.

With small properties—less than four rental units—it's best to have the tenants mail the rental checks directly to the owner. With a four-unit rental or larger, however, the resident manager needs to handle rental income for the owner. Monthly reports (see the sample forms in appendix) are submitted to the owner and are necessary for efficient accounting and ready reference. These reports include a summary of rents (income) collected and bank deposits made (optional, depending on whether the manager or the owner makes the deposit).

Each entry on the summary of rents (income) collected should include the apartment number, rent-paid date and due date, amount paid, and type of income (such as rent, cleaning fee, key deposit, or security deposit). And whenever the manager receives tenant income, it should be recorded on a triplicate form of a rent receipt. One copy is kept on file by the manager, one copy is given to the owner, and the third copy is given to the tenant if he or she requests it.

Major expenditures, such as replacing carpet or a hot-water heater, should be handled only by the owner and billed directly to him or her. This will reduce the temptation for a manager to pad expense bills or receive kickbacks from salespeople. Often you can save on supplies when you buy them in volume or have an established commercial account at major suppliers such as Lowe's or Home Depot.

Once you have a qualified and responsible manager caring for your building, you'll find that an occasional monthly supervisory visit is all that you need to make. On such visits, you can make major decisions, such as whether to undertake expensive repairs such as replacing the carpet in a unit. In addition, during these visits, you can pick up the collected rent and any paperwork from the manager and inspect the premises. Thus the joys of being a landlord can be enriched by having a responsible manager, avoiding the headaches and hassles many amateur owners experience through slipshod management practices.

Noteworthy: The Perils of Being an Absentee Landlord

One time when I was teaching a session of *Investing in Real Estate*, I was discussing the pitfalls of being an absentee landlord, and one of my students told the class the following story: "While I was in Hawaii for two years, I responsibly turned over the management of my rental home to a local Realtor. After about four months, the Realtor called me in Hawaii and said the tenant had moved out. Meanwhile, I never received any rent for about six months. Then I phoned one of my neighbors who lived near the rental home and asked him to take a look at the property. He called me back the next day and said that the house was, in fact, occupied and that the same people who had been my original tenants when I moved to Hawaii were still there. Obviously, the Realtor thought I would never check up on the so-called vacancy, and he was keeping the monthly rent owed to me for himself."

You should be aware that the scenario in the preceding example is a common ruse crooked property managers use to cheat absentee landlords out of their hard-earned rental income. This is why you always should inspect your properties, in particular the vacant units, at least once every month.

Furnished versus Unfurnished Units

Whether you supply the furniture in your rental units depends on whom you intend to market to. If, for example, you intend to operate a boarding house and rent to college students, it will be necessary to supply adequate furnishings. Or if you own small studio-type apartments that tend to attract transient clientele, then supplying furnishings would be advantageous. And, of course, you can then charge more in rent for the use of the furniture. If you do, however, it will be your responsibility to maintain and insure it from theft and fire damage.

The problem with furnished units is that they attract a transient clientele, which creates a lot of turnover. A rented home completely furnished is very easy to get up and move away from. On the other hand, a home for which the tenants supply all their own furnishings requires much more of an effort to move in and out of. Invariably, once tenants take the time, effort, and expense to move all their belongings into a home, it's very likely they plan to stay a while.

Appliances

As a rule, I try not to get involved with supplying my tenants with any mechanical appliances such as refrigerators, washers, and dryers. My reasoning: These items are usually expensive to purchase, and like all things mechanical, they will eventually break and will need to be repaired or replaced. And unless you make special arrangements with your tenants, the cost to repair and maintain these appliances will come out of your pocket.

They do, however, make great amenities to feature in your rental units. So if you have the opportunity to purchase these appliances at bargain prices as part of the purchase price of the property you invest in, then by all means, do so. But if you're going to furnish them in your rentals, you should give your tenants the responsibility for the repair and maintenance of the appliances. And this means that your intentions about this matter have to be made perfectly clear to your tenants before they move in, which also means spelling them out in the rental agreement.

Laundry Facilities

If you purchase a multiunit apartment building with nine or more rental units, you have to consider whether you should supply a laundry facility with coin-operated washers and dryers and whether you should purchase or lease the equipment. In smaller buildings—those with eight or fewer units—installing washers and dryers into a laundry room for tenant use would not be economically feasible because the usage would not pay for the cost of the utilities to run the machines.

Should you decide to purchase the coin-operated equipment, the machines would probably pay for themselves within two years. That's the good news. However, you have to maintain the equipment and be responsible for acts of vandalism and the unauthorized removal of coins from your machines.

On the other hand, you could lease your laundry equipment from a reputable rental company. The leasing company would be responsible for supplying and maintaining the equipment while at the same time collecting coins from the machines. Generally, when you lease laundry equipment, the leasing company retains 60 percent of the gross receipts and remits the remaining 40 percent to the owner. If you decide on leasing, be sure that a responsible person oversees the removal of coins from the rented equipment in order to help eliminate the temptation of skimming from the coin boxes.

Utilities and Trash Removal

Tenants who rent detached single-family residences or condominiums should be responsible for paying for utilities and trash removal. Also, most apartment buildings, especially the later models, have separate meters for gas and electricity consumption, and the respective companies bill the individual tenants. But the owner of the building is usually responsible for paying the water bill. When separate meters for each unit are not available for these utilities, the owner must add the cost to the rent. If this is the case, simply get an overall monthly estimate and divide it by the number of units in the complex.

Whenever you can, it's best to have your tenants on a separate electric meter and have them responsible for paying the bill. Otherwise, tenants tend to be more wasteful with their usage of electricity.

The removal of trash from multiunit buildings is best paid for by the owner so as to maintain a cleaner common area around the building and avoid friction with the tenants as to whose responsibility it is.

Attracting Good Tenants

Having good tenants residing in your properties is the essential key to profitable and hassle-free property management. Good tenants always pay their rent on time, have clean living habits, have respect for others, will usually get along with their neighbors, and will properly care for your property. Unfortunately, you also have to deal with the other kind:

the bad tenants, and you have to learn how to screen them out and keep them from residing in your properties.

Avoiding Bad Tenants

Generally speaking, bad tenants are usually associated with being irresponsible and having bad credit. In other words, they're not going to pay their bills, and it's very likely they won't care for your property either. So why bother with them. Bad tenants are a nightmare for landlords and their resident managers, and you don't need the headaches and extra aggravation that go along with having bad tenants occupying your property. Let the other naïve landlords have all the headaches and horrors that go with nonpaying deadbeats who have no respect for someone else's property.

Bad tenants have the following habits:

- They're slow payers, or they simply don't like to pay their rent at all.
- They have little regard for anyone else's property and usually treat it with disdain and leave the landlord with the chore and expense of cleaning and repairing it. Usually their children are just like the parents, and they tend also to be troublesome.
- They are noisy and are always bothering the neighbors and the resident manager or landlord.

So you have to be wary that there's a bunch of potentially bad tenants out there, who have recently been evicted, gone bankrupt, or whatever, who are desperately seeking and need an unsuspecting naïve landlord that will allow them to occupy their property. It's your job—if you want to avoid all the hassles these kinds of people incur—to weed them out. If you're not careful and rent your available unit to an undesirable deadbeat, you will soon wish the unit was vacant! The surest way to financial suicide, or at least a horrendous nightmare, is to continually rent to flaky people who won't pay their rent. There are enough qualified prospects to fill your vacant units; all you have to do is advertise for them and properly qualify them.

Prequalification and Advertising

The weeding-out process begins with your advertising by "prequalifying" your prospective tenants. For example, consider the following sample advertisement: "3-bedroom, 2-bath apartment. $775/month. References required." The mention of "references" will keep many of the bad tenants from calling you to inquire about the available unit. A potentially bad tenant will simply not call you if he or she suspects that you're going to check references, because the references will be bad! People with bad credit know who they are. And they know that most commercial landlords and savvy apartment owners do thorough credit checks. (You'll also do some further weeding out of your prospects later in this chapter in processing the application to rent.)

Advertising for Prospects

The best way to prospect for tenants is to post vacancy signs on the property and place classified advertising in your local newspaper. Vacancy signs must be precise and to the point, qualifying the prospective tenant to a certain degree. For example, your sign might say "Vacancy, 1-Bedroom, Kids OK," or "Vacancy, 2-Bedroom, Adults Only." Stating certain facts about the available unit eliminates a lot of unqualified prospects who are looking for something you don't have. Your vacancy signs also need to be bright (printed or painted in red or yellow) and legible so that they can be seen easily from a passing vehicle. Erect your vacancy signs on either side of your building or post them on the lawn near the busiest street for maximum exposure.

Classified advertising should also be precise and qualifying in order to eliminate unnecessary calls from unqualified people. Good advertising copy achieves *attention*, *interest*, *desire*, and *action* (remember these as AIDA). To get attention, your headline should attract specific prospects. To stimulate interest, the headline should be expanded to offer a benefit to prospects that makes them read the remainder of the advertisement. Arouse desire with good descriptive copy that makes prospects want what you have to offer. Ask for the action by making it easy for prospects to respond to your offer.

Here are some specific ideas for each objective:

- *Attention.* The purpose of the attention heading is to get the reader to distinguish your ad from the numerous other ads in the same column. Some examples are, "Newly Decorated" or "Large 3-Bedroom" or "Free Rent for one month." (This last type of ad could be used in a rental market already oversupplied with available units. Free rent would definitely get more attention than the other ads in the same column.)

- *Interest.* To develop interest, offer a benefit like "quiet country living" or "newly carpeted" or "great ocean view" to entice the reader to finish reading the remainder of your advertisement.
- *Desire.* This will precisely describe what you have to offer. It's the body of the advertisement. Examples are "2-Bedroom, Kids OK, $775," or "1-Bedroom, pet OK, Pool, $750."
- *Action.* The action getter can simply be a phone number that the prospect can call to get more information.

Classified advertising is printed under specific headings, so there's no need to duplicate information that's already available. In other words, you need not state that your apartment is unfurnished when your ad is running under the column "Unfurnished Apartments."

Begin your ad with the location, then the type of unit. For example, under a column heading of "Unfurnished Houses for Rent," you might say:

BILOXI, 2 miles N of I-10, quiet country living,
Large 2br,1ba on 3 acres, kids & pets OK.
References required. $795. Call 555.1212.

By beginning your ad with the location, you qualify prospects right from the start. People usually look for rentals based on areas they want to live in. Anyone looking for a quiet two-bedroom apartment out in the country will respond to this ad; anyone looking for a three-bedroom in a different area—like downtown—will look elsewhere.

After a full description, including any particular features, close the ad with the amount of rent you require and a phone number to call. Stating the amount of rent is important because it enables you, again, to qualify the prospect. If you're charging more rent than the prospect can afford to pay, he or she won't bother to call.

The following was a sample advertisement that proved very effective. It ran in the *Las Vegas Review Journal*, under the section "Unfurnished Condominiums for Rent."

RENT WITH BUY OPTION . . . Spring Mt. & Jones, 3br, 2ba, Neat & clean, beautifully landscaped & decorated, w/tennis cts, pool, Jacuzzi. References. $695. Call 555.1212.

More Prequalifying: Answering the Ad Calls

In many situations, the people calling on whatever it is you have for rent want to know the address so they can drive by and see it. Before you give them enough information to do that, you need to develop some rapport with them and do a little more prequalifying. You want to avoid showing it to people you might not want to rent to—such as people with bad credit or with too many pets). Which brings us to an important issue—discrimination. Federal law prohibits you from explicitly excluding applicants because of their race, religion, sex, ethnicity, national origin, disability, or family status (households with children). But you should also note that federal civil rights law and nearly all state and local fair-housing ordinances exempt owner-occupied properties of one to four units. So those exempt property owners may discriminate without legal penalty.

While you're on the phone with the prospect, find out as much as you can. Ask the following questions: Do they earn enough to afford your rental? How long have they lived in their present address? How long have they worked at their present job? What number of people will occupy the property? Are there any pets? (If you plan to accept tenants with pets, you could require they pay a nonrefundable pet deposit. More about deposits will be discussed later in this chapter.)

Creditworthiness and Conduct

Laws against stereotyping people because of their race, religion, or family status does not mean that you're legally bound to accept tenants who do not meet your standards for creditworthiness and conduct. To the contrary, you have the legal right to refuse to rent to anyone—regardless of protected status—whose rental record, credit history, or income is below your standards. Unlike employers, who are often forced into special hiring standards, landlords are not required to rent to everyone.

So begin by asking certain questions. For instance, someone calls on your ad for a two-bedroom, one-bath unit and says, "What's the address so we can come by and look at it?"

You reply with, "Yes, but first let me ask you a few questions: Tell me the number of people who will occupy the property?"

The caller replies, "Just my husband and five kids."

You think for a moment: (Hmmm . . . seven people in a small two-bedroom and only one bath) and then say, "Are there any pets?"

She says, "Just three dogs, but they're all well mannered and house trained."

And you reply, "I'm sorry, but we don't allow pets."

In this scenario, you prequalified this prospect by asking certain pertinent questions. And by doing so, you saved a lot of time and effort by not showing the unit to someone to whom you have no intention of renting.

How to Maintain Harmony by Profiling Your Tenants

Single adults like to live with other singles. Folks with families usually prefer living in the same apartment building with other folks with kids so that their kids have someone to play with. And senior adults prefer to live with other senior citizens where they're not annoyed by barking dogs and children at play. Therefore, set certain standards if you own a multi-unit building, and don't try to mix the elderly with the young, or singles with families.

Showing and Renting Available Units

At this point, your advertisement is running in the local paper, and vacancy signs are strategically located on the property. Now it's imperative that the vacant unit be ready to be shown, which means it should be neat and clean throughout. If, by chance, you're showing an occupied unit that the occupants will be moving out of shortly, then inform the occupants of your intentions. Request that they keep the unit tidy so that you can show the unit to prospects.

Showing the Unit

While you're showing the unit, point out features of the unit, such as storage, cabinets, view, and so on. Avoid bringing up anything that you might consider to be negative because what may be a negative aspect to some may not be to others.

If they're interested in the unit, the prospects will usually begin by asking the following questions that you should have the answers to:

- What is the square footage of the rental?
- What are the names of the schools in the district and where are they located?
- Where is the closest bus stop, grocery store, and so on?

Rental Applications

Once your prospects have seen the available unit and decided they want it, what's next? Start with the application to rent (see Figure A.1 in the appendix). Have them fill it out completely while you calculate how much money they are required to pay before moving in. This total amount should be the first and last months' rent, along with any required deposits and a cleaning fee. After they have completed the application, be sure to get a minimum of a $100 deposit (the more the better). The deposit can be in the form of a check, cash, or money order. Find out when you can get the balance owing—first and last months' rent, security deposits, and fees—preferably as soon as you can and definitely prior to move-in. Then check the application for any omissions; if there are none, notify your prospects that you will phone them about your decision once you've made some inquiries.

Qualifying the Prospects

From the information on the application, you now have to determine whether or not to accept your applicants as tenants. Again, you're essentially looking for tenants who will pay their rent on time, are clean living, will care for your property, and not be a nuisance. Keep in mind that you're about to enter into a long-term business relationship with these people, and you don't need the headaches associated with bad tenants. Once your prospects become tenants and gain possession of your property, if for whatever reason you want them removed, you must do it by due process of law, which is costly and time-consuming.

The best way to avoid this catastrophic situation is to do some investigating. Telephone a local credit agency and find out what it requires to do a credit check. If the prospects have no credit, then inquire into their rent-paying habits with their past two landlords. It's a good idea to check with the past two landlords anyway; that way you can inquire about their living habits. Incidentally, you can usually discover a lot about people's living habits by observing how they care for their vehicle. It has been my experience that people who take good care of their vehicle will, in most cases, take good care of the home they live in. Conversely, people who drive a dirty, ill-maintained car in almost every case will have dirty and messy homes and won't take very good care of your property.

This observation will also usually hold true for kids. If the children of the family are reasonably well dressed in clean clothes, it would be a good assumption on your part that the parents will also care for other things, such as your property. So, when prospective tenants arrive at your available unit, check out the condition of the car and the children, if any. Later, if you have any doubts about renting to them, let your observations assist in your decision.

Finally, the prospects have to be qualified on their capacity to pay the rent. Similar to the guidelines lenders use, you should do likewise and use the same ratios for paying the rent. The monthly rent should not exceed 28 percent of the tenants' gross income. However, if they have no consumer debt (such as car loans or credit cards), then they can afford up to 33 percent of their gross monthly income.

Drafting the Best Rental Agreement

Although I have included a sample lease for your consideration and use (see the appendix), you need to develop a practical lease that will serve your individual needs. In designing a lease to fit your particular purposes, try to keep your clauses, rules, and contingencies simple. Avoid the lengthy multipage fine-print leases written in lawyer jargon (legalese). Lawyers, of course, will argue that these lengthy leases cover every conceivable contingency no matter what happens. But these overburdened lists of authoritarian dos and don'ts tend to alienate and intimidate tenants, instead of portraying a cooperative business atmosphere.

Your Marketing Strategy

Keep in mind that you have to compete with other landlords, and many of them *do not* accept tenants with pets. A great marketing strategy to attract good-quality tenants is to be lenient in accepting pets. Perhaps allow them one pet, and charge them accordingly. Typically you can do several things to cover inclusion of a pet: One is to charge your tenants a nonrefundable deposit of between $200 and $400; and/or charge them substantially more rent for the addition of one pet. This means that you cannot accept a menagerie of animals, but you could accept one animal as long as it was less than 40 pounds.

When drafting your rental agreement, consider the following issues and clauses for possible inclusion.

Tenant Names and Signatures

All adult tenants and children that will occupy the premises should be named in the lease. Only the adults are required to sign the lease. As a rule, owners should not permit tenants to freely add more or substitute tenants for those moving out. Any new tenants must be fully approved by the owner.

Joint and Several Responsibility

If you rent a unit to more than one tenant, include a *joint and several responsibility clause*. This means married couples too, because divorces do occur. This clause makes every tenant signed on the lease both individually and jointly accountable for all rents owed and for tenant damages.

Often, when this clause is omitted, individual cotenants can claim they're not responsible for the broken window, and they will say, "Collect from Frank because he did it." Or they will say that they're only liable for their half of the rent. You'll find that in most cases, though, Frank has moved out of town. With a joint and several responsibility clause, you have the legal right to collect monies owed from the other tenants.

Guests

Protect yourself against unwanted guests who end up becoming unauthorized roommates (cotenants) by inserting a *guest clause* in the lease. This clause limits both the total number of people permitted to reside in the premises and the amount of time genuine guests can stay. Without this clause, you may show up at the property some day and wonder who the extra people are. (Calling them "guests" is a sneaky way of not listing roommates on the rental application.) When you ask who they are, you're told, "They're guests. Barbara is just down from Michigan for a couple of weeks." When you come back a month later, Barbara's three kids have also taken up residency.

Personal Property Description and Inventory

If you supply any personal property (stove, microwave oven, washer, dryer, refrigerator, blinds, or draperies) with the rental unit, you need to inventory and describe each separate item as a lease addendum. If you can, keep a photograph and a record of the serial number for each item. Without this documentation, it's difficult to prove theft when a vacating tenant takes your new microwave and leaves a piece of junk in its place.

Discounts and Late Fees

To encourage early or on-time payment of rent, some landlords offer their tenants a discount of about $25 for prompt payment of rent prior to its due date. Other landlords discourage late payers by charging a late fee of 4 to 5 percent of the monthly rent amount when the rent is not paid within five days of its due date.

Your use of one of these strategies will let your tenants know that you intend to enforce your collection policies. Be firm in not allowing your tenants to take the discount or sidestep the late charge unless they pay the rent within the specified due dates. If a tenant is a chronic late payer, I try to arrange a new payment date that better matches his or her cash flow needs.

And this brings up another important issue: Never allow tenants to get behind more than five days in their rent without taking action. Initiate the eviction process as soon as local ordinances permit.

Bad-Check Fees

Also as part of your collection policy, you should never tolerate bad checks. If a tenant remits a bounced check, I charge him or her a bad-check fee of $30. And from that point on, I no longer accept checks from the person—only cash (if I'm doing the collecting) or money orders.

Tenant Improvements

You need to keep tenants from making unauthorized improvements on their own accord without your approval. Always include a clause in the lease that requires the tenants to obtain your permission *in writing* before they make any improvements. The purpose of this clause is to prevent tenants from diminishing the value of the property.

The clause is so important that you need to point it out to the tenants when they sign the lease, emphasizing that they must obtain your written permission before they alter the premises in any way. This includes such modifications to the leased property as paint, wallpaper, or any other type of redecoration.

Sublet and Assignment

When tenants are temporarily away from the premises, such as they might be for an extended summer vacation, they may want to *sublet* the unit (rent to another party). Or when tenants permanently move away, they might be inclined to *assign* their lease to another party. To avoid this situation, which is tantamount to having unauthorized strangers you never qualified or approved occupying your property, make sure you include a no-right-to-sublet-or-assign clause in your lease.

Tenant Insurance

Since property owner's insurance covers only the structure of the premises, not the tenant's personal property within, it's a good idea to include a clause that requires the tenants to carry a renter's insurance policy for personal property.

Grounds Care

When you're the landlord of a rented detached single-family dwelling, it's likely you want the tenants to care for the grounds. To make sure they do that, it's important to precisely explain what it entails. To a tenant "caring for the grounds" might mean simply mowing the lawn. To a caring landlord, it usually means keeping the lawn watered, along with caring for all the shrubs and flowers. If you want the tenants to properly care for your property, spell out the duties you expect them to perform.

Landlord Access

Landlords need an access clause in the lease to enable them to conduct periodic inspections, make repairs, show the unit to prospective tenants, and most importantly take care of emergencies (such as mending a broken water pipe or stopping an overflowing toilet). An access clause, however, does not give you unlimited freedom to access the premises any time you please. Tenants deserve a certain amount of privacy, and with this in mind, except for emergencies, landlords should always get the tenants' permission before accessing a rented unit.

Pets

Although the majority of households have a pet, many landlords refuse to accept pets of any kind. Because of this widespread restrictive policy, landlords who do accept pets have the opportunity to command higher rents and a nonrefundable pet fee. Typically you can charge $200 to $400 as a one-time fee for allowing one pet. If you do accept pets, be sure to include a pet-rules clause in your lease. Also, be careful in accepting tenants with more than one pet, and do not accept pets larger than 40 pounds.

Deposits and Fees

You have to consider security deposits for certain items of personal property that the tenants use frequently that usually go with the property. These include such things as door keys and remote-control garage-door openers.

Also, you should charge your tenants certain fees to cover your costs for restoring their rental unit to good condition when they move out of it. Such fees might include a nonrefundable pet fee and/or an apartment cleaning fee to be paid in advance.

Regarding security deposits and fees, you need to address the following issues in your lease:

- The amounts
- When they are due
- The conditions in which the tenants will forfeit all or part of the fees
- If and when the fees will be refunded to the tenants

Not only do you need to spell out this information in your lease, you also need to go over each item with your tenants during the lease signing. Why? Because often tenants have the misconception that they can apply prepaid deposits to rent that they owe at the time of move-out. To prevent such misunderstandings, it is helpful to explain these important money issues.

- *The amounts and when they are payable.* The more you can get in security deposits, the better. As a rule, try to base the amount on what it would cost to restore whatever it is you'll have to replace, plus something for your trouble. Regarding first and last month's rent, always get the full amount in advance prior to the tenants' moving in. Never allow your tenants to pay the security deposit in monthly increments or permit postdated checks. Remember that you're not renting a flophouse run on charity; instead, you're looking for tenants who have the financial capacity and good rent-paying history to lease your desirable property.

- *Conditions of forfeiture.* It's important that your tenants know up front, before taking possession of the property, your forfeiture-of-deposit policy. Again, security deposits cover any damages to the property that the tenants have caused; it does not cover rent that may be due upon move-out. Furthermore, the tenants have to be made aware that if their liability for rent or actual damages exceeds the security deposit, they're responsible to pay the higher amount.

  The best time to do your final inspection is immediately after your tenants have vacated the premises. Do a walk-through inspection with your tenants present. Use the inventory-of-furnishings sheet you prepared when they first moved in to compare the condition of each item and every room (see Figure A.2 in the appendix). Take note of any damage, and estimate the cost.

- *Deposit refund.* Many penny-pinching landlords hold out for 30 or more days before returning a tenant's security deposit. Instead, as a courtesy to your customers, you should refund your tenant's deposits at the end of the final walk-through inspection. They will surely appreciate it, especially when they probably need it for expenses on the new residence.

The Move-In

Before your tenants are given the keys and take over residency of your rental unit, be sure that they have paid, in full, all monies owed to you. If they paid by check, make sure the check has cleared before they move in. The total amount includes the first and last month's rent, cleaning fee, pet fee, and all security deposits. Be sure that the rental agreement is signed and that one copy is available for the tenants. Also make sure each adult tenant has one set of keys, plus written information on whom to call to have all utilities turned on, along with the name and number of the local cable television company. Finally, inform your tenants that you expect the rent to be paid on time and that there is a three-day grace period after which a late fee will be charged.

Inventory of Furnishings

At the time of move-in, have the tenants go through the unit room by room with you. Here the tenants fill out the inventory and mark any comments and return the form to you. Also, they can note any damage to the ceiling, walls, or flooring. (See an example of an inventory-of-furnishings form in Figure A.2 in the appendix.)

Rent Collection

Never allow your resident manager to accept cash for rent or deposits. Only in an emergency should you allow the manager to ever accept cash. However, your on-site managers can be allowed to accept checks or money orders. This helps to eliminate the opportunity of theft or embezzlement of the owner's income receipts.

Checks should be acceptable from your tenants until you receive a bad check. From then on, you should accept only cash or money orders from offending tenants. (The resident manager, though, can accept only money orders). On your monthly inspection visits to your property, you can either collect rent receipts from the resident manager, or you can have him or her deposit the checks. To do this, order a rubber stamp that reads "For Deposit Only [to your account number]" from the printer, and then require the manager to stamp the back of each rent check. The resident manager can then deposit the checks in your bank account.

Occasionally, a tenant will request a receipt for the paid monthly rent. To be prepared for those instances, it's necessary to furnish the manager with a triplicate receipt pad. One copy of a rent receipt can then be available for the tenant, one for the manager, and one for the owner's records.

Reminders to Pay

Also, as part of your collection policy, you need to follow through with reminders to pay the rent if your tenants become delinquent. First issue a three-day reminder when the rent is three days past its due date. When the rent is five days overdue, issue a more forceful five-day notice. (See examples of the three- and five-day reminders in Figure A.4 in the appendix.)

Eviction Procedures for Nonpayment of Rent

Here's another good reason you need to be particular about who rents your property: Lawful actions to evict a deadbeat tenant will bring a judgment only for rent monies, court costs, and moving fees. Cases that go to court will undoubtedly require 30 days or more to remedy. The costs involved, plus additional loss of rent, can be very expensive to an owner when nonpaying tenants move in to your property.

The following procedure is common in most states for the lawful eviction of a tenant for nonpayment of rent:

1. The tenant in default is served with a three-day notice to pay rent or quit the premises. (See Figure A.5 in the appendix.) To ensure proper legal procedure, the person serving the notice should be the marshal, not the owner, or the resident manager.
2. An unlawful detainer is filed with the municipal court clerk, and a summons is issued.
3. The tenant is served with a summons and a complaint.
4. The tenant has the legal right to file against the complaint, pleading his or her case. In that event, a trial is held.
5. The default of tenant is taken and given to the owner.
6. The court issues the writ of possession.
7. The marshal receives the writ of possession.
8. The marshal evicts the tenant.

Budgeting

The successful operation of a rental building will ultimately depend on a carefully planned budget, which the building owner then sticks to without exception. Essentially, the budget is the financial plan for the upcoming years. Income and expenses are projected to provide an overall view of the building's financial well-being.

If you don't properly plan income and expenses, financial disaster is inevitable. Money must be allocated for certain replacement items over the years so that they can be paid for when they need replacing. When owners fail to allocate funds to replace certain items, they defer maintenance. That, in turn, causes vacancies, which, in turn, cause loss of income and further deferred maintenance and eventual loss in value.

Good budgeting sets aside a proportionate allowance for the future replacement of certain expensive capital items, such as carpeting, roofs, elevators, pool equipment, air-conditioners, and furnishings. Thus a contingency fund is set aside each month and held in reserve to replace these capital items when needed.

How much do you set aside each month? It depends on the amount of capital equipment you have. For example, carpeting usually has to be replaced, on average, about every seven years. New carpeting in today's market for a one-bedroom apartment costs about $700. Therefore, you budget $100 per year per apartment (about $8 per month), which is set aside in a contingency fund to replace carpeting. Likewise, a replacement reserve fund must be set up for other capital items as well. By preparing a budget, such as a reserve fund, you'll have money set aside when certain expensive things break down instead of suddenly being faced with a large expenditure and not having adequate funds.

The best way to budget these items is to estimate total outlay for all future expenditures, maintaining the fund for each item in a savings account to use when the money is required. You determine, for instance, that the cost of a new roof is $2,400 and that it will last 20 years. Divide the total cost by the number of months, and the result is the amount that should be budgeted each month. So $2,400 divided by 240 months equals $10 per month allocated for a replacement reserve for roofing.

Expense items such as property taxes and hazard insurance also have to be budgeted if they're not part of your monthly impound account and paid by your lender. Both property taxes and insurance are projected at one-twelfth of the annual bill per month.

As a rule, 5 percent of gross collected rents is usually an adequate amount for all replacement reserves. However, this amount should be increased for additional capital equipment such as a heated pool or spa.

Record Keeping

Proper record-keeping procedures are necessary so that the information will be accessible when needed, especially when your accountant needs it, or if the IRS decides to make a surprise audit. Keeping records is simple when your investments are single-family homes. All you need is a separate 8.5- by 11-inch manila envelope for each home, properly labeled, while keeping all records and expense items inside the envelope. All income collected can be noted on the outside of the envelope, along with addresses of note holders, balance owing on the notes, and initial cost of the property. At the end of each year, you can start a new envelope for the upcoming year.

Multiunit buildings, such as apartment houses, require somewhat more elaborate record-keeping systems, with a separate set of records for each building. Make up file folders and label them "General Records," "Tenant Records," "Receipts and Expenses," and keep these files in a file cabinet. In the general records folder, retain such information as escrow papers, insurance policies, taxes, notes, and deeds. In the tenant record folder, maintain all rental applications, rental agreements, and any other data pertaining to your tenants. In the receipt folder, retain all paid receipts for all expenses related to the building and a copy of all rent receipts. Later you can arrange the expense items chronologically for tax purposes. At the end of the tax year, this envelope should be stored separately for at least five years, just in case you have to verify anything.

Tenant Record on File Card

For each tenant in an apartment building, set up a tenant record on a 5.5- by 8-inch file card, as shown in Figure 10.1. Whenever a tenant makes a payment, record it on the tenant record file card.

Journals of Income, Expenses, and Depreciation

For each multiunit building, keep separate journals in which you post all relevant income and expense data monthly. These journals give you ready access to all current data relating to each property's monthly compilation of income and expenses. The journal of income in Figure 10.2, for example, takes into account all income collected for each unit in the building

Figure 10.1 Tenant Record on File Card

Address ______________________________ _____ Key Signature ______________________

Orig. Move-In Date ____________

Lease Dated _____ Exp. __________

Tenant Tel. No. ______________

Date Due	Date Paid	Receipt Number	Paid to Noon	Amount Paid	Security Deposit	Cleaning Fee	Key Deposit #	Base Rent	Refrigerator	Furniture	Parking	Month to Month	Additional Occupancy	Other Fireplace & Dishwasher	Air-Conditioner	Utilities	Total Rent	Balance Due	
Deposit																			
Rent																			

BLDG. # ________ APT. ________ FL. PL. ________ CLR. ________ NAME ________________ DATE DUE ________

Figure 10.2 Journal Income Record

Monthly Income Record Page # ________

Address ______________________________

Year __________

Unit	Jan.	Feb.	Mar.	Apr.	May	June	July	Aug.	Sept.	Oct.	Nov.	Dec.
1	400	400	400	400	400							
2	390	390	390	390	390							
3	425	425	425	425	425							
4	275	275	275	275	275							
5	415	415	415	415	415							
6	460	460	460	460	460							
7												
8												
Total	2,365	2,365	2,365	2,365	2,365							

Figure 10.3 Journal Expense Record

Expense and Payment Record

Address ______________________ Year # __________ Page # ______

Date	Paid to	Paid for	Total Paid	Mortgage Principal	Mortgage Interest	Tax	Ins.	Mgt.	Repairs and Maint.
1. 1/1	bank	1st mort	760.00	122.80	427.20	120.00	90.00		
2. 1/1	Smith	2nd	125.00	92.40	32.60				
3. 1/3	hdwr.	parts	9.60						
4. 1/7	water	water	56.71						
5. 1/8	muni ct	evict	21.00						
6. 2/1	bank	1st mort	760.00	124.06	425.94	120.00	90.00		
7.									

each month for the entire year. Figure 10.3 takes into account all the expenditures that have been made for the building. So all the income and expense receipts you keep in file folders are also posted in these journals each month. Anything you do not have receipts for can be recorded from your checking account record.

Once you have completed an entire page on the expense journal, as shown in Figure 10.3, total each column and bring the balance forward to the next sheet. Then start posting your subsequent entries. After you have posted your last expenditure for the year, total the last sheet, and you'll have your year-end income and expense totals for each category of your building.

Be careful not to post on your expense record such capital items as carpeting or a new roof. These are depreciable items, not expenses, and they are considered improvements to the property. (See Figure 10.4 for a sample depreciation record.)

Figure 10.4 Depreciation Record

Location and description of capital improvement: 3750 Raymond, Los Angeles, CA: A 19-unit apartment building.

Date acquired:	January 1987
New or used:	Used
Cost or value:	$220,000
Land value:	$40,000
Salvage value:	0
Depreciable basis:	$180,000
Method of depreciation:	Straight line
Useful life:	27.5 years

Year	Prior Depreciation	Depreciation Balance	% of Year Held	Depreciation This Year
1987	0	$180,000	100%	$6,545
1988		173,455	100	6,545
1989		166,910	100	6,545

Depreciation Records

Depreciable items are property or equipment that have an extended useful life and are considered to be improvements to the property. Some examples are carpeting, elevators, linoleum floors, roof replacements, and swimming pools. Each of these items must be depreciated on a separate depreciation record form, such as the sample shown in Figure 10.4.

Annual Statement of Income

This statement brings together all relative income and expenses for the year and shows the net profit or loss of the subject property. Figure 10.5 provides an example. Notice how depreciation, not an out-of-pocket expense, is deducted last for tax purposes. The bottom line is the net profit or loss shared with the IRS.

Figure 10.5 Annual Income Statement

Location: 3750 Raymond, Los Angeles, CA. Year: 1988

Annual income:		
Rent	$28,471	
Laundry	629	
Total annual income		$29,100
Expenses:		
Interest	$8,410	
Taxes	4,800	
Utilities	1,812	
Service, repairs	321	
Pest control	120	
Insurance	850	
Management	1,800	
Total expenses		18,113
Net income (before depreciation)		10,987
Less depreciation		−6,545
Net income for tax purposes		4,442

Repairs

Part of no-hassle management operations is avoiding some of the nuisances that are common to managing residential rentals. If you make the tenant responsible for the cost of repairs up to a certain limit, you will elude many of the menial calls for certain minor repairs.

In the sample rental agreement shown in Figure A.6 in the appendix, under line 19, "Tenant Maintenance," it says, "If a professional service call is required, the tenant shall pay the first fifty dollars ($50) of the total repair bill." Having this clause in your rental agreements helps to make your tenants more responsible because they know they have to pay for repairs, so they'll be more inclined not to recklessly break things. And it will help to reduce troublesome phone calls to the landlord requesting repairs.

Chapter Lessons

Remember that the devil is in the details—be as concerned about small details as about big ones. People will pay more to live in an immaculately maintained building than an average building. Make people want to be in your building because of your eye for detail. You can impress existing and prospective tenants in the following ways:

- Making sure that the premises, inside and out, are as clean as they can be at all times.
- Putting money into items that offer services for the occupants. Rather than providing just a building, provide some customer services as well such as having the building superintendent be available to receive packages delivered for the tenants.
- Providing tenants with a Jacuzzi tub, a steam unit in a stall shower, and a granite-looking countertop in the bathroom.
- Installing special lighting in the bathroom for putting on makeup, great-looking cabinets and a center island in the kitchen, lots of storage space throughout the unit, and a well-thought-out design.
- Providing a resident manager or superintendent who is readily available and has a customer-service attitude.

The key to hassle-free property management is learning how to avoid many of the hassles that naïve property owners have to deal with. Your objective is to rent *only* to qualified, responsible people who pay their bills on time including the rent and who know how to take care of your property. All you have to do is learn how to weed out the bad tenants and abide by some simple rules outlined in this book.

Investigate: Find out who your potential tenants are. Make them fill out a rental application, and call a past landlord or two. Also, get a thorough credit check on them. Check out the car they drove up in. If the inside is messy and uncared for, that's usually a telltale sign of how they will live in your rental.

The Four "Nevers" of Successful Property Management

1. Never be an absentee landlord. Why? Because there are too many ways unscrupulous property managers can embezzle your hard-earned income when you cannot personally inspect your properties on a regular basis.
2. Never allow your resident manager to collect cash from tenants. You don't want to give anyone the opportunity to embezzle or steal your rent receipts.
3. Never accept tenants without thoroughly checking their credit history and getting references from their past landlords.
4. Never allow tenants to occupy the premises until they have paid all monies due in full.

11

How to Retire on Your Realty Investments

Key Points

- *How to utilize your built-up equity*
- *The future demand for rental housing*
- *How to retire "on the house"*
- *An income for life*

Investment in real estate can give you varying degrees of wealth during your lifetime; it all depends on how much effort, time, and money you devote to the wealth-building process. Consider several investment scenarios. In the first scenario you buy just one house for $110,000 with a $10,000 down payment, along with a $100,000 mortgage for 30 years. Based on a very conservative annual rate of appreciation of 4 percent, look what happens to your small initial investment. At the end of 30 years, the mortgage is paid off and you own the home free and clear of any debt. So your small down payment of $10,000 has grown exponentially to a value of $300,140.

But 4 percent is a very conservative estimate of future appreciation in real estate, given all the economic factors mentioned earlier that affect the value of real estate—such as, expanding growth in households who will need a home, an insufficient supply of habitable land, and regulatory constraints on home builders. Look what happens to the purchase of a similar house when more realistic rates of appreciation are factored in over 30 years. At 5 percent, you can expect a $10,000 down payment to increase $491,350. And at 6 percent, a similar down payment would grow to $589,350 in equity.

In the other scenario, instead of just one house you buy three or four houses in the next 10 years, and at retirement, your net worth could easily be in the range of $300,000 to $1 million or more. Assuming only modest increases in rents—at 4 percent annual appreciation, $1,000 rent today is equivalent to $2,000 in 18 years—the income from those rental houses could reach $10,000 per month. And that kind of income is generated from owning only three or four rental properties. Imagine how much income you could earn with even more rentals!

How to Utilize Your Built-Up Equity

All right, you say. I've got all this equity in my home. What do I do with it?

You have several alternatives. If all you have is one home, and you're living in a high-priced real estate market—such as the coastal areas of northern and southern California—you could downsize (trade down) and relocate to a more affordable part of the country. For instance, home owners in the San Francisco area, where the average home is selling for $740,000, are selling their homes, taking their huge tax-free profits, and buying comparable homes for less than a third of the price in places like nearby Sacramento or Las Vegas, Nevada. They can live off the substantial price differential between the two homes, which is often in the neighborhood of $500,000.

Better yet, instead of accepting all cash for the sale of your home, consider an installment sale and take back a purchase-money mortgage, and just watch all the interest-bearing income roll in for the next 20 or 30 years.

Still another way to tap the equity in your home is to refinance and pull out tax-free cash, as outlined often in this book. You can use the proceeds to retire on, or do whatever you wish, including investing in rental property.

How to Retire "On the House"

In the "plant a seed and watch it grow investment plan," your first investment in real estate is the foundation from which most of your future wealth will be derived. Think of it as the root from which other plants will grow. The plants, of course, are additional realty investments that grow from the root. When you make wise improvements and properly care for the original property, after several years of appreciation and paying down the mortgage, you can refinance and pull some or all of the cash out of the built-up equity and reinvest it in additional properties. Think of "pulling cash out" as akin to taking cuttings from the original plant that has now begun to blossom. The cuttings will be planted, and they too will blossom if you give them the same good care that you gave the original plant. And their blooms will come in the form of huge amounts of property appreciation and increased rental incomes.

Then, several years down the road when you've accumulated substantial equity in the second or third properties you've invested in, do the same thing over again. You do it by renting out the house you're presently living in and moving into the property you just purchased. In this way you can utilize the benefits of owner-occupied financing (lower interest rates and smaller down payment requirements) discussed in Chapter 4.

Later on, when you've accumulated more appreciation and paid down the mortgage, you can refinance one of your properties and use the proceeds to do the same procedure over again. When you properly utilize the success-proven guidelines outlined in this book, you could, realistically, retire comfortably on your income-producing realty holdings alone.

The Future Demand for Rental Housing

Predicting the long-term future of inflation, social security, or stock prices is virtually impossible. But as long as America's population and economy continue to expand, there will always be great demand for rental housing. Real estate ownership will provide the most reliable and secure strategy to long-term wealth for the average person.

You'll also enjoy the benefit of knowing your capital investment is safe in real estate. Even in the midst of a general nationwide recession, property values endure and the landlord's rent receipts remain relatively stable. During these slumping periods of economic activity, the housing supply tightens as the number of home and apartment-building construction projects declines. Economic downturns—which are usually associated with high unemployment and tight credit markets—also have a propensity to draw more households toward renting and away from homeownership. And when the economic downturn finally reverses itself and the economy begins to grow and flourish, rising employment, more income, and general prosperity puts more pressure on an already tightened housing supply. The end result is higher rents and more appreciation in real estate values as more households, along with an expanding population, strive to occupy a tight housing market.

An Income for Life

Many real estate owners who had the wisdom to hold on to their properties over the long haul are now, in the autumn of their life, able to live off their net rental income. Today's realty investors have to be patient and realize that real estate is a much better long-term investment than a short-term one. That means that over the long haul, you'll make more money holding on to real estate than you will "flipping" it in a quick sale. That's because you gain from the long-term effects of appreciation and mortgage pay-down. But when you sell a property soon after you have bought it, you not only have to find another investment to invest the proceeds in, you will likely have to pay taxes on the capital gain.

Newcomers who recently purchased rental property have to be patient too and realize that income property purchased today with a small down payment is unlikely to net an immediate positive cash flow. But as time passes, all the factors we discussed earlier that increase the demand for real estate go to work: The property steadily appreciates, and the rents are gradually raised, which results in greater income and more equity gained in the property. So the lesson in a nutshell is: Buy all the real estate you can when you're young; then enjoy all the great tax-free income benefits when you're older.

12

How to Avoid Paying Too Much in Taxes

Key Points

- *Homeowners' tax savings*
- *Rules for vacation homes*
- *Rules for home offices*
- *Rules for passive losses*
- *Capital gains*
- *Depreciation*
- *Reporting rental income and deductions*
- *Summary of important book highlights*

We've already discussed many of the great benefits of owning real estate—such as the advantage of earning high returns through the use of leverage and equity buildup from paying down your mortgage—and these are all wonderful wealth-building benefits. But these are all for naught if you can't protect what you've earned. And that's what makes investing in real estate so beneficial—you can virtually shelter most of what you earn in real estate from the crippling effects of paying too much in taxes.

Of course, you could decide to shun this field of taxation and hand over your financials to a tax professional. That would be a shortsighted mistake that could cost you thousands, if not hundreds of thousands, of dollars. Instead, you should at least learn the basics so that you can discuss tax strategies with an adviser. This way you're at least familiar with the subject and can plan a smart tax-shelter strategy that can legitimately reduce or avoid the IRS's share of your hard-earned gains.

Keep in mind that the federal tax code is very complex and constantly changing. In writing this particular chapter, I have endeavored to simplify some of its complexities and make a condensed, brief overview of important tax issues that are related to real estate investing. In doing so, I am merely trying to inform you about the basics of tax law and many of the tax benefits of owning real estate so that you can anticipate the tax effects of various alternatives. For more specifics about a particular tax subject, please seek the advice of a competent tax professional.

That said, let's begin a brief overview of the federal tax law basics with regard to real estate investing and how you can reduce your tax liability.

Homeowners' Tax Savings

Since tax laws heavily favor homeownership, homeowners benefit by enjoying several tax-saving advantages. The greatest advantages exist in relation to your owning your primary residence because you can deduct your payments of mortgage interest and property taxes. And when you sell your home, under certain limitations, you have the benefit of earning capital gains without paying taxes on them.

Mortgage Interest Deduction

The combined mortgage interest deduction on your residence and a second home is set at a maximum of $1 million ($500,000 if married filing separately). You may deduct interest on the borrowed funds to acquire the residence plus the interest on the cost of any improvements. If you later refinance and pay off the old mortgage and have excess money, you cannot deduct the interest on the excess money unless it's used for property improvements or for educational or medical expenses. You can also deduct interest paid on a home improvement loan up to $100,000.

Points are sometimes deductible too. The points you pay to originate a loan are deductible in the year the loan was funded if you pay them up front. They're not deductible, however, when the points are borrowed as part of the loan amount. Points on VA and FHA loans are not deductible.

Capital Gains Exemption

The IRS allows an exemption of up to $250,000 ($500,000 married filing jointly) on the capital gains tax of a principal residence when it's sold if the owner lived in the property for at least two of the past five years.

Noteworthy

As part of the *Tax Reform Act of 1986*, the capital gains exemption was limited to $125,000; it applied only to those 55 years or older; and it could be used only once in a lifetime. Fortunately, though, times have changed, along with the federal tax code. Nowadays, there is no age restriction on the capital gains exemption, and there is no limit on the total number of times you can use the exclusion. There is, however, a limit of one capital gains exclusion every two years.

Less-Than-Two-Years Exclusion

In some circumstances, you can get a reduced tax exemption if you lived in the residence for less than two years. If the reason you sold the residence is a medical condition or a job relocation that qualifies for the moving-expense deduction, then you qualify for a partial exemption based on the number of qualifying months. For example, if you had a $60,000 sale profit and lived in the home only one year of the five years you owned it, then $30,000 would be exempt from capital gains taxes.

The IRS also lists seven other qualifying conditions for a partial home-sale exemption after less than two years of ownership and occupancy:

1. Death of the homeowner, co-owner, spouse, or family member
2. Job loss that qualifies for unemployment compensation
3. Legal separation or divorce of an owner
4. Damage to the home by disaster, war, or terrorism
5. Multiple births from the same pregnancy
6. Condemnation of the home by a government agency
7. Change of employment that causes insufficient income to pay for ordinary living expenses or the mortgage

Downsize and Reinvest

You could also benefit from this form of tax exemption if you own a home with substantial equity. This particular strategy is ideal for those living in high-valued areas—where median home prices can exceed half a million dollars—and the kids are gone and they want to downsize. You can sell that large, expensive house and put that hard-earned equity to work. Take your tax-free equity (up to $500,000) and use part of it for a down payment on a lower-priced replacement home, along with several income properties. Finance all the newly acquired properties with low-cost 30-year fixed-rate mortgages. And with property appreciation, mortgage pay-down, and regular rental increases building your net worth, in the not-too-distant future you could be very rich and, more important, financially independent.

Rules for Vacation Homes

According to federal tax law, a vacation home can be a condominium, an apartment, a detached single-family dwelling, a house trailer, a motor home, or a houseboat. But unlike your personal residence, the profits from the sale of a vacation home will be taxed as capital gains, with no exclusions. If, however, any rental income was earned from the vacation home, you're allowed to deduct some of the expenses incurred, according to the following rules:

- If the vacation home is rented for fewer than 15 days, with the exception of mortgage interest and property taxes, you cannot deduct expenses allocated to the rental.

- If the vacation home is rented more than 15 days, you have to determine whether your personal use of it exceeds a 14-day or 10 percent time test (10 percent of the number of days the home is rented). If it does, then the home is considered as your residence during the year, and rental expenses are deductible only to the extent of gross rental income. Thus, if gross rental income exceeds expenses, the operating gain is fully taxable.
- If the vacation home is rented for 15 days or more but your rental usage is less than the 14-day/10 percent test, then you're not considered to have made personal use of it during the year. In that case, expenses in excess of gross rental income are deductible. Past tax court cases have allowed loss deductions when the owner showed little personal use of the vacation home and proved to have purchased the home with intent of earning a profit on resale.

Rules for Home Offices

When you use a part of your home exclusively for business purposes—such as managing your rental properties—you may be able to set up a tax-deductible home office. To qualify as a home office, the area must be used *exclusively* and on a regular basis for work (a room where the kids watch television or where your spouse reads while you use the telephone does not qualify).

If you qualify for a home office, you're allowed to deduct a proportionate amount of expenses that relate to your work. These include pro rata amounts for depreciation, telephone, insurance, computer, and office furniture. But if your rental properties don't show a taxable income (because of allowable deductions), home-office expenses *cannot* be deducted in that year. However, these home-office expenses can be carried forward and used as needed deductions in the following years,

Rules for Passive Losses

These rules apply to realty investors who report taxable income in excess of $100,000 annually and to those investors who take no active role in the operational or managerial decisions that affect their properties. For all intents and purposes, passive-loss rules were enacted to disallow high-income earners from sheltering their incomes through depreciation deductions—a common practice of the wealthy before the Tax Reform Act of 1986.

Exemption from Passive-Loss Rules

Taxpayers in the real property business are exempt from passive-loss rules. This category includes owners of income property, converters, real estate agents, contractors, and property managers. The advantage of being in this category is that you may use rental property tax losses to offset the taxable income received from other sources, including wages, commissions, royalties, dividends, and interest.

But there's a catch: You're required to work a minimum 750 hours per year in a real estate–related business or trade, the equivalent of slightly over 14 hours per week. Also, the majority of the personal services work performed each year must be within the definition of a real property business or trade. You couldn't, for instance, simply go out and get a license to sell real estate and automatically qualify for this preferred tax status. (For specifics, talk with your tax professional.)

Capital Gains

The preferential treatment of capital gains has traditionally been one of the most important tax benefits for realty investors. Under present law, the amount of taxes depends on the holding period of the asset. If the property is held for at least one year, gains realized in the sale of real property are taxed at a maximum rate of 20 percent (18 percent if held for at least five years) and possibly lower depending on your tax bracket.

If you're in the 15 percent ordinary income tax bracket and you held the property for at least one year, your capital gains are taxed at 10 percent instead of the 20 percent used for those in the higher tax brackets. Under similar circumstances except that you have held the property for at least five years, your capital gains are taxed at 8 percent.

Depreciation

Depreciation is the "no-cash-out-of-pocket expense" income property owners are allowed to deduct from rental income because they don't have to write a check for it. Essentially it's a bookkeeping entry, and it is commonly referred to as the *tax shelter benefit* of owning rental property, and it's added to other deductible expenses, such as repairs and maintenance.

The IRS presumes that buildings, their contents (such as carpeting, heating equipment, and elevators), and certain improvements (fencing, outbuildings) wear out over time. Thus, you're allowed to deduct a depreciation allowance to reduce your taxable income to compensate for this wear and tear.

Deducting the Value of the Land That a Depreciable Building Sits On

To calculate your depreciable cost basis, you first have to deduct the value of the land your depreciable building sits on because the land is not depreciable. Thus, if you buy a property for $240,000 and its lot value is $60,000, your original depreciable basis is $180,000. Tax law permits a useful life of 27.5 years. Divide $180,000 by 27.5, and the result is $6,545. That's the amount of depreciation—much like repair or maintenance expenses except that you don't write a check for depreciation—that you can deduct each year from your taxable rental income.

Calculating Depreciation

Say, for example, that similar to the preceding situation, you invest in an income property valued at $240,000 and it yields a net operating income (rent less operating expenses) of $15,000 annually. Your mortgage payments total $12,000 a year, of which $11,000 represents deductible interest and $1,000 equals equity payoff. We already determined a yearly depreciation allowance of $6,545. Here's an illustration of how the numbers work:

Net operating income	$ 15,000
Less mortgage interest	−11,000
Income before depreciation	4,000
Less depreciation	−6,545
Taxable income after depreciation	(2,545)

From the preceding illustration, after deducting all out-of-pocket expenses, you earned a profit of $4,000, but because of depreciation, you showed a net loss. This net loss of ($2,545), in most cases, can be deducted against wage income (or other sources)—thus, the tax shelter benefit of depreciation.

Reporting Rental Income and Deductions

Rental income and related expenses are reported on Schedule E of your federal tax return. Begin with your gross rental income received for the year, and then deduct expenses such as loan interest, property taxes, maintenance costs, and depreciation. The result is the net profit that is added to your other reported income (such as wages). If you realize a loss, you can reduce the amount of your other reported income within certain limitations. (See preceding section on passive-loss rules.)

To reduce your tax liability, it's important that you keep detailed records for all allowable deductions. Again, maintain a separate envelope for every property, and keep all expense receipts in it that you believe necessary to operate the property. The following are the most common allowable deductions:

- *Depreciation.* Be sure to take advantage of this no-cash-out-of-pocket expense. It's the tax shelter benefit of income property ownership.
- *Real estate taxes.* Property taxes are deductible, but special assessments for installing sewers, paving roads, or other public improvements may have to be depreciated or added to the cost of the land.
- *Maintenance expenses.* These are service-related costs that pertain to such items as repairs, pool maintenance, lighting, heating, gas, electricity, water, and telephone.
- *Interest expense.* This includes the payment of interest on mortgages and other indebtedness related to the property.
- *Travel expenses.* These may include the cost to travel to and from your properties to show vacancies or do repairs.
- *Management expenses.* All fees paid to a professional management company are deductible. You cannot, however, pay yourself a deductible salary unless the property is owned by a separate partnership or corporation. However, you are allowed to pay your spouse or other family members and then deduct these expenses.

Tip

Regarding travel expenses, you're only allowed to deduct the actual business portion of your travel costs. To avoid problems with the IRS, it's important to segregate business mileage from other driving you might do at the time you actually use the car. Keep a logbook in your glove box and get in the habit of jotting down mileage at the beginning and end of each business-related trip.

- *Accounting and legal expenses.* This category includes the cost of filing tax returns and maintaining financial records, along with the costs involved to evict a tenant and negotiate a lease.
- *Advertising expense.* This includes the cost of newspaper advertising, rental signs, and Web sites.
- *Insurance.* This category includes the cost of premiums for fire and casualty loss.
- *Capital improvements.* Here it's important to know the difference between *repair expenses* and an *improvement.* Only incidental repair costs and maintenance costs are deductible against rental income. Capital improvements and replacement costs are treated differently. Improvements or repairs that add value or prolong the life of the property are considered capital improvements and may not be deducted, but they may be added to the cost basis of the property and then be depreciated. For example, the cost to repair the roof of a rental property is considered an expense and is deducted against rental income. However, the cost to replace the entire roof is considered an improvement (adds value and prolongs the physical life of the building) and is therefore added to the cost basis of the property and then depreciated.

Summary of Important Book Highlights

Remember that in order to get the most out of your real estate investments, you have to think long term. By holding on for the long haul, you'll be able to take advantage of all the great benefits that investing offers. These include price appreciation, equity buildup as your mortgage pays down, regular increases in rental income, and a great tax shelter.

Remember too, that when you become a specialist in a particular field of real estate, you gradually gain expertise and become more efficient and knowledgeable in your chosen field of endeavor. This way you become an expert at what you do. For newcomers to real estate, becoming a specialist at detached single-family houses is a wise choice. And don't forget all the key guidelines to making a superior investment. If you follow them, you can rest assured that your realty investments will reward you year after year.

And keep in mind that when it comes to financing real estate, don't be lured by all the fancy offerings the commercial lenders can tease you with. The best choice for the long haul is always a traditional 30-year fixed-rate mortgage.

Finally, as you gain experience in real estate, you'll learn that a little money can buy a lot through the proper use of leverage. But to be successful and optimize your profits, you have to also abide by the following: Be very selective in the property you buy, be a great negotiator, and foremost among them all, find quality tenants to live in your cherished properties. So get started now. By starting small, always adding value with selective, appealing improvements and generating more income, continually reinvesting that additional income into more property, and repeatedly saving and adding value to your other properties, you can quickly build a magnificent net worth.

In closing, I want to wish you much success with your real estate investing. And I want you to know that I enjoy hearing from my readers. So if you have the opportunity, please contact me on my Web site: Andrewmclean.net

Appendix: Useful Forms

The forms in this section are for your use as you see fit, including duplicating each page on any type of photocopying equipment.

Application to Rent

You can overcome many of the hassles frequently encountered by novice landlords by properly qualifying your prospective tenants. Conscientious people with good credit who will care for your property are a valuable asset. They're the good seeds in your garden of prosperity; you only need to weed out the so-called bad seeds to help ensure that your property management experience will be a fruitful one.

After your prospects have filled out the rental application (see Figure A.1), review it carefully, making sure that everything is legible and complete. Be certain the names are correct because later on if Jim Jones skips the premises, he will be easier to trace with his complete name of James Anthony Jones. If more than one person will occupy the premises, get the names of all the adults, and make everyone responsible for rent payments.

Be sure too that each adult includes his or her social security number. It is essential to conducting a thorough credit check.

Employment information is also very important. You definitely want to qualify the prospects on their ability to pay the rent. As a general rule of thumb, a range of 28 to 33 percent of gross monthly income can safely be paid in rent—28 percent if there are some other debt obligations and 33 percent if there are not. If your prospects qualify based on their salary, then at a more appropriate time you should verify their employment. A simple phone call to the employer is sufficient.

Credit Check

Credit bureaus need a complete name, date of birth, present address, and a social security number to conduct a complete credit check on your applicants. You can also do some checking with the applicant's last landlord or second from last landlord by phoning him or her and inquiring about the applicants' conduct and rent-paying habits.

Multiple Tenants

You will have added protection by having each adult tenant sign all the documents of the rental agreement. This way the parties are jointly responsible, and if one of the lease signers skips out, it may still be possible to locate one of the others.

Figure A.1 Application to Rent

Name of first applicant ______________________

Date of birth ____________ Social security number ____________

Present address ______________________

City ____________ State ____________ Zip ________

Home phone ____________ Work phone ____________

Unit to be occupied by ______ adults and ______ children and ______ pets

Driver's license state ______ Driver's license # ____________

Current landlord/mgr's name ____________ Phone ____________

Why are you leaving? ______________________

Previous address ______________________

City ____________ State ____________ Zip ________

First applicant's employer ______________________

Address ____________ Gross monthly pay ________

Position ____________ How long? ________

Credit references: Bank ________ Account # ________ Type ________

Other active reference ______________________

In an emergency contact ____________ Phone ____________

City ____________ State ____________ Zip ________

Name of spouse/second applicant ______________________

Date of birth ____________ Social security number ____________

Present address ______________________

City ____________ State ____________ Zip ________

Home phone ____________ Work phone ____________

Driver's license state ______ Driver's license # ____________

Current landlord/mgr's name ____________________ Phone ______________

Why are you leaving? ____

Previous address ____

City ___________________________ State ________________ Zip __________

Second applicant's employer ___________________________________

Address ______________________________ Gross monthly pay ___________

Position ___________________________________ How long? ___________

Credit references: Bank __________ Account # __________ Type __________

Other active reference ____

In an emergency contact _____________________ Phone ______________

City ___________________________ State ________________ Zip __________

List all major vehicles, including RVs, to be kept at the dwelling unit. Include make, model, year, and license plate number for each.

Vehicle 1 ___________________________ License plate # ________________

Vehicle 2 ___________________________ License plate # ________________

Vehicle 3 ___________________________ License plate # ________________

I (we) declare that the above information is correct and that I (we) give my (our) permission for any reporting agency to release my (our) credit file to the undersigned landlord solely for the purposes of entering into a rental agreement. I (we) further authorize the landlord or his or her agent to verify the above information including but not limited to contacting creditors, both listed herein or not, and present or former landlords.

First applicant _______________________________ Date ________________

Second applicant _____________________________ Date ________________

Inventory of Furnishings

An inventory of furnishings should accompany the rental agreement for each individual unit (see Figure A.2). This form is used essentially to identify items supplied by the owner, such as the refrigerator, stove, washer, dryer, or couch, and to denote the present condition of each item. Later, if a lawsuit is necessary, the completed form can be used to support a claim of damage, excluding reasonable wear and tear, against the security deposit. The tenants may counter that the damage was there before they moved in. Except in cases of gross and negligent damage, such a defense is difficult to overcome without proper documentation.

At the time of move-in, have the tenants go through the unit room by room with you. Have the tenants fill out the inventory and mark any comments and return the form to you. If the space provided for comments is too small, have your tenants make any additional comments on the reverse side of the form and note, "See reverse side."

Figure A.2 Inventory of Furnishings

Rental unit address ____

Tenant ______________________ Tenant ______________________

Date of inventory ____________, 200__.

Room	Item	Comments	Condition at Move-Out

Tenant agrees that the above information is an accurate inventory and description and assumes the responsibility for these items in the dwelling unit as of _______, 20__.

Move-in

_______________ Date ______

_______________ Date ______

Move-out

_______________ Date ______

_______________ Date ______

Tenant Record on File Card

For multiunit buildings, keep tenant records on 5.5- by 8-inch cards. Each card is a ready reference of all monies paid by and due from tenant, a description of the apartment type, including the floor plan (FL PL) and the color of carpet (CLR), plus other important tenant information (see Figure A.3).

Figure A.3 Tenant Record on File Card

Address ______________________ _____ Key Signature ______________________

Orig. Move-In Date ______ Lease Dated _____ Exp. ______ Tenant Tel. No. ______					Security Deposit	Cleaning Fee	Key Deposit #	Base Rent	Refrigerator	Furniture	Parking	Month to Month	Additional Occupancy	Other Fireplace & Dishwasher	Air-Conditioner	Utilities	Total Rent	Balance Due	
Deposit																			
Rent																			
Date Due	Date Paid	Receipt Number	Paid to Noon	Amount Paid															

BLDG. # ________ APT. ________ FL. PL. ________ CLR. ________ NAME ______________ DATE DUE ________

Reminders to Pay Rent

Efficient landlords should never tolerate their tenants' being delinquent in paying their rent. You need to react predictably and immediately to nonpayment of rent when it's due. Slow-paying tenants usually react to this predictability and make the rent a high priority on their list of payments. Normally there is a three-day grace period after the rent due date. If the rent is not received within three days of the due date, action has to be taken by the owner and/or manager.

Collection experts agree that a first notice should be sent within five days of the due date, and a second notice after seven days. Use forms such as those in Figure A.4. If your slow-paying tenant has a history of continued delinquency, a Notice to Pay or Quit the Premises could be used in favor of the second notice. (For a sample of a pay-or-quit notice, see Figure A.5.)

Figure A.4 Reminders to Pay Rent

Three-Day Reminder to Pay Rent

To ______________________________ Date ____________________

____

Just a reminder that your rent was past due on ____________________.
According to the terms of your Rental Agreement, rent more than ________
days past due requires a late-charge payment of $ ____________________.
We would appreciate your prompt payment.

Thank you,

____
Owner-manager

Figure A.4 (*Continued*)

Five-Day Reminder to Pay Rent

To ______________________________ Date ________________

____

Your rent is now past due as of __________________. As of this date, the past due rent and late charges total $ _________________.

You must settle this account, or our legal options will have to be considered. Therefore, please act to remedy this matter immediately.

Thank you,

____

Owner-manager

Notice to Pay or Quit

The pay-or-quit notice, Figure A.5, gives the tenant three days from date of the notice to pay all monies in default or move out of the premises. You issue this form to the tenant only after you have attempted to procure the amount owed through other means, such as the three- and five-day reminders.

Note: Exercise caution in using a pay-or-quit notice because laws on this matter of eviction procedure vary throughout the country. This particular form may not conform to the laws in some states. If this is the case in your state, seek the appropriate form at a reputable legal stationery store or consult with an attorney who is familiar with the eviction procedure in your area.

Figure A.5 Notice to Pay Rent or Quit the Premises

To ______________________________________ Date ____________________

You are hereby notified that the rent for the period ______________, 20 ____, to __________, 20 _____, is now past due. As of this date, the total sum owing including late charges is $ ___________. Unless the sum is received within three days of this dated notice, you will be required to vacate and surrender the premises.

If it becomes necessary to proceed with legal action for the nonpayment of rent or to obtain possession of the premises, as per the terms of the Rental Agreement, you will be liable for recovery of our reasonable attorney's fees and expenses. You will also be liable for any additional rent for the time you are in possession of the premises.

____

Owner-manager

Rental Agreement

For your convenience, I have included a sample residential lease agreement in Figure A.6. You can modify this document for your needs, but note that both the tenant and owner or manager must initial any handwritten changes on the printed lease. Take special notice of the following three items that are an integral part of the rental agreement:

- *Term, section 1.* In this section you need to specify whether the agreement is on a month-to-month or year-to-year basis. Be wary of committing to more than one year. If you do use a term of one year, specify graduated rent increases every twelve months that can be tied to the rate of inflation, such as 1.5 times the CPI. This will protect your from losing money due to inflation.
- *Rent, section 5.* Make sure the amount of rent is spelled out and that a late fee is specified, which is commonly 5 percent of the monthly rent.
- *Tenant maintenance, section 19.* Under this heading note the clause “If a professional service call is required, the tenant shall pay the first $50 of the total repair bill.” This is part of your hassle-free management program. By making the tenant partially responsible, he or she will be less likely to bother you or the resident manager with menial repairs and will be more conscientious about caring for the rental unit.
- *Pets, section 3.* In this section of the agreement, use the clause that’s best suited for your particular unit and cross out the clauses you are not using. Then be sure both the owner and the tenant initial the change to the lease at precisely where you’ve made the change on the document.

Figure A.6 Residential Lease Agreement

Residential Lease Agreement

This agreement made this date, ______________________________, is between ______________________________, the "owner," and ______________________________the "tenant."

Description of leased property. Witnesseth, the owner, in consideration of the rents to be paid and the covenants and agreements to be performed by the tenant, does hereby lease unto the tenant the following described premises located thereon situated in the city of ____________________, county of ____________________, state of ____________________ , commonly known as ______________________________
____
____.

1. **Term.** The term of this lease shall be ______________months, beginning ______________________ and ending ______________________, 200___. It is agreed that if the tenant is transferred or moved by an agency of the federal government or a branch of the military, this agreement becomes null and void and deposit money will be refunded after inspection of the unit.

2. **Security deposit**. The owner acknowledges receipt of $______________ as security for the tenant's fulfillment of the conditions of this agreement. The owner shall return the security deposit to the tenant, without interest, within thirty (30) days after the tenant has vacated the premises if:
   a. The lease term has expired or the agreement has been terminated by both parties;
   b. All monies due the owner by the tenant have been paid; and
   c. The premises are not damaged and are left in their original condition, except for normal wear and tear.

Tenant's initials ____________ Owner's initials____________

The tenant shall deliver possession of the premises in good order and repair to the owner, with all outstanding bills paid upon termination or expiration of this agreement. The security deposit may be applied by the owner to satisfy all or part of the tenant's obligations for the unit. Such act shall not prevent the owner from claiming damages in excess of the deposit.

The tenant may not apply the security deposit to any rent payment without the approval of the owner.

3. **Pets.** No animals, birds, or pets of any kind shall be permitted. (Or subsection a or b, may be used, in which case, the the previous sentence needs to be crossed out.)
   a. One dog not to exceed 40 pounds is permitted, but the tenant must pay a nonrefundable pet fee of $400.
   b. One cat not to exceed 15 pounds is permitted, but the tenant must pay a nonrefundable pet fee of $400.

4. **Possession.** If there is a delay in delivery of possession by the owner, the rent shall be abated on a daily basis until possession is granted. If possession is not granted within two (2) days after the beginning of the initial term, then the tenant may void this agreement and receive a full refund of any deposit. The owner shall not be liable for damages for delay in possession.

5. **Rent.** Rent is payable monthly in advance at a rate of $__________per month during the term of this agreement, on the 1st day of each month, at such place that the owner may delegate.

6. **Late charge.** If rent is paid after the 5th day, a charge of $30 shall be added. After the 15th day, collection shall be turned over to the Justice Court and a $60 charge shall be added for court expenses. Any other court-related expenses shall be added.

7. **Returned-check charge.** If a returned check has to be collected, $30 shall be charged to the tenant for collection. If the check is not made good by the 15th day, it shall be turned over to the District Attorney's office for collection and a $60 fee shall be added.

Tenant's initials ___________ Owner's initials__________

8. **Lease renewal.** Either party may terminate this agreement at the end of the initial term by giving the other party thirty (30) days' written notice prior to the end of the term. If no notice is given, this agreement shall be extended on a month-to-month basis, with all terms remaining the same until terminated by either party upon thirty (30) days' written notice.

9. **Use.** The premises shall be used so as to comply with all state, county, and municipal laws and ordinances. The tenant shall not use the premises or permit it to be used for any disorderly or unlawful purpose or in any manner so as to interfere with the neighbors' quiet enjoyment of their homes.

The premises shall be used for residential purposes only and shall be occupied by only the following persons:

____
Name Age Social security number

____
Name Age Social security number

____
Name Age Social security number

____
Name Age Social security number

10. **Sublet.** The tenant shall not sublet the premises or assign this lease without the written consent of the owner.

11. **Utilities.** The tenant shall pay for all charges for all water supplied to the premises and pay for all gas, heat, electricity, and other services supplied to the premises, except as herein provided: ______________________________.

12. **Property loss.** The owner shall not be liable for damage to the tenant's property of any type for any reason whatsoever except where such is due to negligence by the owner.

13. **Smoking.** Smoking shall not be allowed on the premises.

Tenant's initials ___________ Owner's initials___________

14. **Failure of the owner to act.** Failure of the owner to insist upon strict compliance with the terms of this agreement shall not constitute a waiver or any violation. Also, the waiver of one breach of any term, condition, covenant, obligation, or agreement of this lease shall not be considered to be a waiver of that or any other term, condition, covenant, obligation, or agreement or of any subsequent breach thereof.

15. **Fire.** If the premises are made uninhabitable by fire not the fault of the tenant, this agreement shall be terminated.

16. **Indemnification.** The tenant agrees to indemnify and release the owner from and against all loss, damage, or liability incurred as a result of:
    a. The tenant's failure to fulfill the conditions of this agreement;
    b. Any damage or injury happening in or about the premises to the tenant's family, friends, relatives, visitors, invitees, or such person's property unless caused by the negligence of the owner.
    c. The tenant's failure to comply with any requirements imposed by any governmental authority; and
    d. Any judgment, lien, or other encumbrance filed against the premises as a result of the tenant's action.

17. **Cumulative remedies.** All remedies under this agreement, or by law or equity, shall be cumulative. If a suit for any breach of this agreement establishes a breach by the tenant, the tenant shall pay to the owner all expenses incurred in connection herewith.

18. **Notices.** Any notice required by this agreement shall be in writing and shall be deemed to be given if delivered personally or mailed by registered or certified mail.

19. **Tenant maintenance.** The tenant agrees to maintain the premises in good repair and to cause no damage to, or allow anyone else to cause any damage to, the premises. If a professional service call is required, the tenant shall pay the first fifty dollars ($50) of the total repair bill. The owner shall enter the premises each month to replace the central air-conditioning unit filter.

Tenant's initials __________ Owner's initials__________

20. **Alterations and additions.** The tenant shall not make any alterations, additions, or improvements to said premises without the owner's written consent. All alterations, additions, or improvements made by either of the parties hereto upon the premises, except movable furniture, shall be the property of the owner and shall remain upon and be surrendered with the premises at the termination of this lease.

21. **Entry.** The owner or his or her representatives shall have the right to enter the premises at all reasonable times to inspect, make repairs to or alterations to, or show the premises to prospective purchasers, tenants, or lenders. The tenant shall not be entitled to abatement of the rent by reason thereof.

22. **Insurance.** The tenant understands and agrees that it shall be the tenant's own obligation to insure his or her personal property.

23. **Abandonment.** If the tenant removes or attempts to remove property from the premises, other than through the usual course of continuing occupancy, without having first paid the owner all monies due, the premises may be considered abandoned and the owner shall have the right, without notice, to store or dispose of any property left on the premises by the tenant. The owner shall also have the right to store or dispose of any of the tenant's property remaining in the premises after the termination of this agreement. Any such property shall be considered the owner's property and title thereto shall vest in the owner.

24. **Mortgagee's rights.** The tenant's rights under this lease shall at all times be automatically junior and subject to any mortgage debt that is now or shall hereafter be placed on the premises. If requested, the tenant shall promptly execute any certificate that the owner may request to specifically implement the subordination of this paragraph.

25. **Sale of property.** All parties understand that if the owner agrees to sell the property during the term of the lease, the lease and future rents shall transfer to the new owner.

Tenant's initials ___________ Owner's initials__________

26. Entire agreement. This agreement and attached addendums constitute the entire agreement between the parties, and no oral statements shall be binding.

The undersigned tenant(s) herby acknowledge receipt of a copy of this lease.

____Tenant(s)/date

____Tenant(s)/date

____

Tenant's phone Social security number

____

Tenant's phone Social security number

____Owner/date

Owner's phone ____________________

Please mail rent to:

____

____

____

Tenant's initials __________ Owner's initials__________

Bibliography

Associated Press. "Boom areas expand in U.S." *Mississippi Sun Herald,* May 6, 2005, page C7.

Mauer, Robert. *One Small Step Can Change Your Life: The Kaizen Way.* Workman Publishing, New York, June 2004.

McLean, Andrew, and Gary Eldred. *Investing in Real Estate,* 4th ed. Wiley, New York, 2003.

Ross, George H., with Andrew James McLean. *Trump Strategies for Real Estate: Billionaire Lessons for the Small Investor.* Wiley, New York, 2005.

Index

Index

Index

Index

Index

Index

Index

Index

About the Author

Andrew J. McLean, a graduate of Michigan State University and distinguished author of 15 books, says, "This is the book I wish was available when I began investing in real estate. If this book had been available in the early 1970s and if I had utilized the lessons given in it, I could have negotiated far better deals, I could have arranged better financing, I could have made more lucrative investments, and I honestly believe, as I reminisce, that I would have earned significantly more money."